When Your Spouse Comes Out
Comes Out
A Straight Mate's Recovery Manual

When Your Spouse Comes Out
A *Straight Mate's Recovery Manual*

Carol Grever, MA
Deborah Bowman, PhD

Routledge
Taylor & Francis Group
New York   London

For more information on this book or to order, visit
http://www.haworthpress.com/store/product.asp?sku=6046

or call 1-800-HAWORTH (800-429-6784) in the United States and Canada
or (607) 722-5857 outside the United States and Canada

or contact orders@HaworthPress.com

The Haworth Press, Taylor & Francis Group, 270 Madison Avenue, New York, NY 10016.

PUBLISHER'S NOTE
The development, preparation, and publication of this work has been undertaken with great care. However, the Publisher, employees, editors, and agents of The Haworth Press are not responsible for any errors contained herein or for consequences that may ensue from use of materials or information contained in this work. The Haworth Press is committed to the dissemination of ideas and information according to the highest standards of intellectual freedom and the free exchange of ideas. Statements made and opinions expressed in this publication do not necessarily reflect the views of the Publisher, Directors, management, or staff of The Haworth Press, or an endorsement by them.

Identities of individuals discussed in this book have been changed to protect confidentiality.

Library of Congress Cataloging-in-Publication Data

Grever, Carol.
     When your spouse comes out : a straight mate's recovery manual / Carol Grever, Deborah Bowman.
          p. cm.
     Includes index.
     ISBN: 978-0-7890-3628-5 (hard : alk. paper)
     ISBN: 978-0-7890-3629-2 (soft : alk. paper)
     1. Bisexuality in marriage. 2. Closeted gays—Family relationships. 3. Coming out (Sexual orientation)—Psychological aspects. 4. Gay men—Relations with heterosexual women. 5. Lesbians—Relations with heterosexuals. 6. Marital conflict. 7. Self-help techniques. I. Bowman, Deborah, PhD. II. Title.

HQ1035G74 2007
306.872—dc22

2007017272

We dedicate this book to straight spouses the world over, and to their gay partners and families. Their perilous personal journey is examined with compassion and understanding on these pages, with the hope that the stories and principles offered here will support healing and full recovery for all. We are especially grateful to the generous individuals who allowed us to interview them and to use their experiences to help others on this path.

ABOUT THE AUTHORS

Carol Grever, MA, experienced the shock of her husband's disclosure of his homosexuality after they had been married more than thirty years and had reared their two sons. She successfully recovered through all the stages of straight spouse healing, and has become a recognized spokesperson on straight spouse matters with wide exposure on network radio and television, including *The Oprah Winfrey Show.* She is a former English professor and staffing company owner. Ms. Grever's published work includes *My Husband Is Gay: A Woman's Guide to Surviving the Crisis,* which has been translated into Thai and Spanish, and a collection of poetry, *Sun of a New Dawn.*

Deborah Bowman, PhD, is a Professor at Naropa University in Boulder, Colorado, where she founded the Transpersonal Counseling Psychology program and the Wilderness Therapy program. She teaches a variety of courses, including Gestalt Awareness, Professional Identity, and Group Dynamics and Leadership. Dr. Bowman has worked with a wide range of issues as a clinical psychologist with over 19 years of experience in private practice. She is a director and professional trainer with the Boulder Psychotherapy Institute offering courses in Gestalt Therapy, the Child Within, Creativity, and Dreamwork. Dr. Bowman's work has appeared in the *Gestalt Review.*

CONTENTS

Foreword

How I wish this book had been available when my husband came out to me in 1972. We had been married only seven years when he fell in love with Gordon. In retrospect, I was lucky, for John told me before he told anyone else and before he became sexually active. Although I experienced the feelings of other straight spouses, I believe his initial honesty allowed us to become and remain close friends after our divorce two years later.

In the early 1970s there seemed to be nowhere for me to turn for help—no books, no PFLAG (Parents, Families, and Friends of Lesbians and Gays), no Straight Spouse Network. Even the medical and therapeutic communities were ignorant about what I was going through. My physician recommended a therapist who wanted me to free-associate about my father to figure out why I had chosen a gay man to marry. A divorce recovery group I attended told me I was lucky my husband hadn't found another woman. I was isolated and in crisis, believing I was the only person to whom this had ever happened.

Grever and Bowman's fine book not only relieves the isolation that occurs when a spouse comes out but offers hope for recovery. Through the stories of others they outline the practical ways straight mates can survive the experience and move forward into their own lives. They never make it seem easy, for it isn't, and they honor the suffering, the struggles, and the pain. They acknowledge that the process of recovery will not be quick and that the length of time needed will vary with each person. They are also clear that there is not one way through this experience. Every straight spouse must find his or her own path.

I think many of us in this situation would prefer to be given a definite plan to follow that will assure us of recovery. This manual does not provide a simple method, however, for the authors know that true healing is complicated and multilayered and ultimately comes from

When Your Spouse Comes Out
Published by The Haworth Press, Taylor & Francis Group, 2008. All rights reserved.
doi:10.1300/6046_a

the inside out. Instead of step-by-step instructions, the book provides the straight spouse with a map of the territory that includes vital information, suggestions, encouragement, and the stories of others who have survived and thrived. Even thirty-four years after my husband came out to me I discovered new insights into my own experience by reading *When Your Spouse Comes Out.*

Most helpful to me was the authors' emphasis throughout the book on the process of *awareness, insight, and action. Awareness* is the willingness to attend to our own feelings, thoughts, and needs. *Insight* follows when our awareness allows us to more accurately perceive the external environment. This clarity allows wise choices that lead to *action.* The process they outline encourages us to recognize our own power in the healing process. The authors cannot tell us what to do, but they can help us discover for ourselves our own road to recovery. Although I did not have their help those many years ago, I now understand how in the middle of crisis I found the courage to leave therapy.

After many sessions with the therapist I had been sent to, I became *aware* that the process we were engaged in was not helpful. We were getting nowhere, and I began to feel like I was drowning. This awareness led me to *insight.* I was able to accurately assess the situation: By her identifying as central what she believed to be my choice to marry a gay man, she was ignoring my fear, anger, and pain. I realized I was with the wrong therapist and I took *action.* I terminated our relationship. I have since recognized that moment as a turning point in my own recovery. I had discovered that I knew what I needed and had the power to make my own choices.

Over years of working with straight spouses, both individually and in support groups, I have witnessed the power of learning the process of *awareness, insight, and action.* Grever and Bowman, through stories, reflection questions, and suggested activities, walk their readers through this process in relation to fear, isolation, shame, self-doubt, anger, and grief. Gently, without judgment, they encourage us to name our experience, gain whatever understanding we can glean from it, and use that knowledge to make wise choices. By presenting the common and almost universal experiences of the straight spouse in this way, they avoid giving us a formula for healing.

In the section on grief I was excited to discover the term *complicated grief.* I have always known that I grieved the loss of my marriage and the future we had planned and that I had experienced all the stages of the grieving process. Still I wondered why it seemed so hard, and I wondered why I had thought and later heard a number of other straight spouses say, "This would have been easier if he had died." Grieving a loss through death is a *simple grief,* by no means easy and certainly painful, but grieving with most deaths is public and does not involve shame and isolation. If our spouses had died we could have mourned them surrounded by love and support.

Grever and Bowman also provide information about other factors that lead to the experience of complicated grief, such as the effects the coming-out process has on family and friends. Because one partner is lesbian or gay, others are forced to face or deny their own feelings, prejudices, and misunderstandings about homosexuality—and neither path is easy. Therefore, many friends desert both partners. However, if the reason for the divorce is kept secret, undeserved blame is often aimed at the straight spouse, further complicating the grieving process. If there are children in the marriage, their needs and feelings must also be considered. Their reactions to discovering the homosexuality of one parent and the possible loss of their family as they know it will add to the grief of both parents.

Multiple losses and unresolved earlier losses also compound the grief of the straight spouse. I recognized myself in this section of the book. My husband and I had no children, so I did not have to deal with that complication, but my grief was intensified by the death of my father three years earlier, which I had never fully grieved; the judgment of my mother that caused us to be estranged for many years; and the loss of my in-laws, who wanted nothing more to do with me. Because John wanted his homosexuality to be a secret, I cut myself off from all my friends. I was in the throes of complicated grief for years. How good it is now to have a name for what I was experiencing so many years ago. I am reassured that what I felt then was normal, for I wondered at the time if I were going crazy.

The final chapter of this wonderful book is congruent with all that has gone before. The authors do not tell us how we might be positively changed by this wrenching experience, but they do tell us that our lives can be transformed. They share stories of people who have survived, healed, and are now thriving in their newly created lives. Grever and Bowman point out some common themes in these stories, such as recognizing one's own needs, living with new goals, and nourishing the spirit. They end the book by giving us an image of healing that speaks to the wonder and power of the human spirit.

This book will touch readers in different ways. I picked out the sections that spoke to me. You will find different stories and themes to clarify your experience and assure you that you are not alone. There is something within these pages for everyone who has experienced the coming out of a spouse, as well as for those who love us, and for the professionals who will be there to help us. Grever and Bowman have given us a compassionate and professional manual for recovery. As you read, allow their words and wisdom to nurture your spirit and give you hope.

Reverend Jane E. Vennard
Senior Adjunct Faculty
Iliff School of Theology
Denver, Colorado

Preface

"I'm gay!"

When a heterosexual's mate utters these words, life changes in an instant and will never, ever be the same for either partner. My husband of thirty years disclosed his homosexuality and we suddenly found ourselves in a completely different realm. With his one sentence, "I have homosexual tendencies," we both plunged into a crisis of identity. In those first few days, my mind was pummeled by disbelief, disorientation, fear, confusion, deep sadness, and anger. Trust was gone. Our plans evaporated. I was in shock.

The ensuing months were chaotic, as my husband and I worked together and separately to understand how our lives would go on. Could we remain married? Would the family be destroyed? Were we trapped in secrecy? Would we die with AIDS? Could I meet my deepest needs, married to a gay man? Would I grow old in lonely isolation? Hundreds of unfamiliar questions battered my heart and mind.

That initial crisis was the beginning of a more complicated journey. Awash with doubts, we took many months with many false starts to work our way through waves of confusion. Even with counseling and our best efforts it took a long time to begin healing, to gain clarity, and finally to regain an optimistic sense of self. After four years in the closet of secrecy, we finally did separate and divorce amicably, but the emotional toll was heavy.

Afterward, I engaged these hard-won personal lessons to encourage others who found themselves in mixed-orientation marriages. I wrote *My Husband Is Gay: A Woman's Guide to Surviving the Crisis* (Grever, 2001), revealing my experience and that of twenty-five other heterosexual women whose husbands had come out. Focusing on that event and its immediate aftermath, it was a crisis survival handbook for straight wives. Courageous, determined women demonstrated on its pages that a mixed-orientation marriage need not be entirely destructive to either spouse, despite initial shock and inevitable suffering.

When Your Spouse Comes Out
Published by The Haworth Press, Taylor & Francis Group, 2008. All rights reserved.
doi:10.1300/6046_b   *xv*

The hopeful thesis of that book touched thousands of women in many countries of the world. Though all the straight spouses who shared their stories in *My Husband Is Gay* are Americans, women in other cultures identified with our experiences and understood. The book was first distributed in English-speaking countries and I heard from women in the United States, England, Australia, South Africa, and Canada. Later, when it was translated into Thai and Spanish, other women who grew up in vastly different cultures in Asia and Central/South America also responded. In matters of the heart, we are all the same. People everywhere need love and security, deep trust within the family, and a safe environment for their children. Though our languages and geographic locations differ, our shared hurt is familiar and we comfort each other via the Internet. Worldwide exploration of this subject proves that homosexuality is a fact of life in all cultures, and when gay people marry heterosexuals, the entire family experiences radical challenges and upheaval.

My Husband Is Gay explored the *initial crisis* faced by straight wives, but early survival is only the beginning of a longer process. Key questions begged answers. Are there differences in the way men and women perceive the straight spouse situation and deal with it? What pitfalls do people encounter and how do they bridge them? What are typical long-term challenges? What are some secrets of successful rebuilding and renewal? I continued interviewing straight spouses to find answers, finding more than forty role models who have walked this path, some for thirty years or more. Their stories provide answers that can help overcome other deep personal losses as well, whether related to mixed-orientation relationships or not.

This new book, *When Your Spouse Comes Out,* explores long-term healing for both male and female straight spouses. Co-author Dr. Deborah Bowman, a clinical psychologist and professor in the Transpersonal Psychology Department at Naropa University, brings both counseling experience and academic training to the project. She identifies patterns in the case studies and provides a psychotherapist's insight into straight spouses' unique challenges. She also offers solid therapeutic techniques for self-help. This book attempts to identify practical steps that successful individuals have taken to keep this one traumatic event from ruining their future. True stories prove that, for most, the damage is not irreparable. When they are fully healed, straight spouses can craft a new reality and thrive again.

The book is divided into three sections. In Part I, *Ground—Understanding Contrasting Patterns,* characteristic but diverse reactions to the coming-out event reveal typical stages of coping by straight spouses. Case studies form a mosaic of personal experience, creating the ground for Part II, *Path—Self-Healing Guide for Straight Spouses.* This middle section defines and interprets immediate personal challenges, family and social concerns, and long-term obstacles. Here, Dr. Bowman's expertise sheds light on core issues. Finally, Part III, *Fruition—Thriving After Crisis,* examines the fruition of lessons learned on the straight spouse path and suggests some secrets of transformation.

True stories of straight mates, both male and female, illustrate chapters in each section. Spouses' experiences are told in their own words, taken from the interviews. Only their names have been changed to protect their identity. Their direct quotations are integrated into the text and are *designated by italics,* rather than by endless quotation marks. The intent is to have these real people speak directly to the reader. Questions and activities at the end of each chapter reinforce the ideas presented and help readers apply others' wisdom to their own situation. The result is a self-directed path to recovery, which can be used individually or in the context of a support group. Two appendixes contain a compilation of exercises and activities plus additional resources.

Whether facing the straight spouse challenge isolated and alone or working with a support group as a participant or facilitator, you are invited to join us on this journey to renewal. We invite you into this poignant world of real people whose former lives were shattered. Watch and learn how some picked up their broken pieces and transformed them into wholeness. Practice their techniques for healing. Their triumphs and disasters and shared wisdom can point the way toward greater awareness and the possibility of thriving after crisis.

Part I: Ground—
Understanding Contrasting Patterns

Chapter 1

Three Straight Spouse Stories

Crisis brings out the best and the worst in people. How do some individuals rise above dramatic misfortune, while others succumb? Discovering common factors that allow people to survive, grow, and thrive after a major life trauma is the purpose of this book. All of the people here have two characteristics in common: All are heterosexuals whose mates are homosexual. All experienced fundamental confusion when their partners came out of the closet.

Sorting out the factors leading to later happiness is a difficult task because of the personal variables at work. The fortunate ones have support and intrinsic emotional tools to help; others are overwhelmed by too many demands on too many fronts and they cannot cope. To recognize key differences between those who triumph and those who do not, it is useful to begin by looking closely at examples that illustrate contrasting responses. They speak for themselves.

When Your Spouse Comes Out
Published by The Haworth Press, Taylor & Francis Group, 2008. All rights reserved.
doi:10.1300/6046_01

A VICTIM: "JUST GETTING BY"

Kim was only eighteen when her sister introduced her to Mike. He owned a small restaurant at the time and was a *very manly,* well-built Vietnam veteran, four years older than she. She was instantly attracted to him. *He was gorgeous!* she remembers. After seeing each other for just a few months, the two were married.

A virgin, Kim had been reared in a repressive home where the topic of sex was never discussed. She was totally naive. *I had no experience, no idea what's normal.* Moreover, her sense of self-worth had been damaged very early. She was molested at age five and had always *felt unworthy.*

Her narrow upbringing in a midsized Iowa town offered no preparation for what Kim later confronted. Girlish romantic dreams about marriage soon soured as the lack of communication from her childhood home translated into her marriage. She and Mike had a very distant relationship, which deteriorated even more after the early months. In all of their eighteen years of marriage, they were unable to talk about their feelings or disappointments. There was little sex, even at first, and virtually none after their three children were born. As a result, Kim felt totally undesirable and unfulfilled. She felt *rejected, day in and day out. After the three children, there was never any more sex or closeness. We never could communicate about anything except the kids.*

Kim became more disillusioned as the years passed. Mike was unwilling to take part in any social activity. *Everything was a lie. I had to cover for him not wanting to be involved at church or with other couples or family gatherings.* Even Mike's connection with his own children deteriorated. *He was a great father to the kids until they hit the age of seven or eight, then he was an absentee parent.* Kim's loneliness intensified. After seven years without any loving warmth, she had obsessive thoughts. *I even thought about how it would be to be raped! It might not be so bad . . .*

Sick with loneliness and thinking there was something really wrong with her, Kim went into counseling. It was the first time she had discussed her marital unhappiness with anyone. About that time, she found a gay porn magazine hidden under the rug in the family basement. At first she thought it belonged to her fourteen-year-old son but learned that it was her husband's. When Mike minimized the incident and made excuses, Kim wanted to let it go. *I really didn't want to know,* she says. But that incident was the introduction to her life's biggest challenge.

A couple of months later, just before Thanksgiving, Kim came back to the house at an unusual time on a workday. She had returned home from her job as a teacher's assistant to retrieve a notebook she'd forgotten that morning. Though she'd left the front door unlocked, she was surprised to find that it was bolted from the inside. After Kim knocked and rang the doorbell repeatedly, Mike finally opened the door, wearing only his bathrobe. She thought it strange that he was still at home at midmorning. He acted nervous. Kim walked through the house, pretending to look for the notebook, and Mike kept walking right behind her. *Things just didn't feel right. Something odd was happening.*

When Kim went into the downstairs den, she noticed that the television set was on and there were two coffee cups on the table in front of the couch. As she turned to go upstairs, some impulse pushed her instead to the spare bedroom. She switched on the light. Suddenly a young man raced past her, almost running into her as he rushed up the stairs. All she remembers seeing clearly was the side of his face and the earring in his ear.

Now she couldn't deny Mike's secret gay life. Everything, all the odd details, began to make sense. Surprisingly composed, she knew what she had to do. *I calmly walked back upstairs and told Mike to have all his belongings out of the house by 3:30 when the kids and I got home. Then I went back to work.*

Kim's calmness didn't last long. *I began to freak. I called my counselor.* The therapist gave Kim two instructions: Send Mike to a doctor for an AIDS test, and make an appointment that very night for a counseling session. Kim's father had died just before these events, and her mother suffered from life-threatening heart disease. Thoroughly shaken herself, she couldn't risk shocking her mother with the reason for her separation from Mike. In a similar effort to protect her children, she gave them just a tiny piece of the truth. She told them only that Mike had committed adultery. When Mike's blood test showed he was HIV positive, the concealment became more complicated. Hiding the whole truth created a health danger for her unknowing family and made Kim's cover-up even more difficult.

Kim suffered under the terrible burden of hiding Mike's homosexuality and probable AIDS. Her days were filled with lies, both explicit and implied. Add to that her financial worries. After she gained full custody of her three young children, she was in a panic about how to support them, particularly since her husband had left her with debts and five years of back taxes to pay. *I didn't know how I could support and raise these kids without help.* Kim's emotional struggle was exacerbated by her fear of violence. *Mike was possibly suicidal, and he threatened to kill me if I ever told anyone.* She was trapped.

Kim's emotional stability steadily eroded over the next three years. With less than the whole story, her children pressured her to forgive his "adultery" and to reconcile with Mike. Her hardships and stress increased. She blamed God and considered suicide. Desperately needing support, she told her troubles to two friends at work and then confided in her brother. A few close friends at her church then learned the truth. For a while the church provided her enough emotional security to keep going.

Kim lived in this hell of half-truth, fear, and deep instability until a violent incident finally forced the issue. Mike's brother had come to stay with Mike and his live-in boyfriend. The three disagreed and there was a bloody fistfight. Kim's youngest daughter, Connie, just ten years old, happened to be at the house. She saw it all. After the police came to break up the battle, Connie cleaned up the mess—including the blood.

Now Kim had to act. AIDS was a looming menace. She couldn't keep Mike's homosexuality and the AIDS danger from her children any longer. They had to know everything. But she just didn't have the strength! If she told the kids herself, she was afraid Mike would kill her. With some guidance from her minister and counselor, she devised a convoluted plan for a close friend whom the children loved and trusted to divulge the details. She also arranged for a counselor and the youth minister from the church to be present to help ease the blow. At the moment they were hearing the truth, Kim had a strange feeling of perfect peace. She hoped her kids at last would understand and sympathize with her dilemma.

But Kim's difficulties were far from solved. She was amazed and angered when her children saw their father as the injured party, particularly later, when he developed full-blown AIDS. Again, Kim felt rejected.

In the midst of her struggles, one enlivening activity cheered Kim. She attended an aerobics class, and then several. Her mind cleared and her body benefited when she sweated out her frustration. Her muscles grew firm and she liked the changes she saw in her mirror. Trimming down and sculpting her petite figure, she began to feel somewhat better about herself. (Even now, her best advice is, *Use your anger to get in shape physically and at least raise your self-esteem by looking good!*) *When my twentieth high school reunion was announced, I had been working out for three years. My counselor insisted that I attend . . . and I was very much sought after by guys that never gave me the time of day.* That was Kim's brightest time in a very dark period. She felt good about herself for the first time in years, but even that pleasure ended. After she suffered a serious knee injury that required surgery, she was no longer able to continue her strenuous fitness classes. It was a depressing loss.

Sixteen years have passed since Kim found Mike with his male lover. She has suffered extreme self-recrimination *for being so naive and not leaving him years earlier.* She says, *My self-esteem was so low that I thought my family and church friends were paying people to be nice to me. I felt like hiding in a closet and I didn't want to be acknowledged or noticed.* At one time her anger bred violent thoughts. *I remember hoping my husband would try to force his way into my house and I could shoot him legally.*

Unfortunately for Kim, her pain and anger have not subsided in these ensuing years. She did fall in love with another man and experienced genuine sexual pleasure some time after her divorce from Mike, but the relationship didn't last and she blames herself (despite the fact that this man was an alcoholic). She feels robbed of her best years. When asked the long-term effects of her marriage to a gay, she lists a litany of woes: *I think the kids no longer trust adults. I don't feel I deserve somebody who can really commit or am afraid to risk it. I don't trust men. I am always tense and afraid of change or risk. I won't allow myself to be happy; I sabotage it. I am self-destructing.* Clearly, she is still in trouble.

Kim describes her present state as *just getting by.* She tries to be kind to Mike, who is now homebound by his illness, and says, *For the kids' sake I am good to him. I now feel sorry for him and try to help him. Sometimes I take him dinner. I am still angry because he let me live a lie, even though I supported him unconditionally for so long.*

I hope to be able to pray for him. She goes in and out of depression and takes antidepressant drugs—as well as numbing herself with alcohol and marijuana. After her knee surgery, she also became addicted to painkillers. She says she is *hooked on the adrenalin of roller-coaster emotions.* Her money problems worsened. She works two jobs and spends weekends alone smoking dope, drinking, and becoming more and more friendless and isolated.

Kim recognizes that her methods of masking pain are leading to disaster, but she seems powerless to change her ruinous path. She's still a victim, nearly two decades after discovering Mike's homosexuality. In spite of her dilemma, she clings tenuously to her faith and a slim hope that things will change. *Without God, I would have given up and possibly destroyed myself completely.*

Kim's downhill path is somewhat extreme. She struggles with difficult limitations: alienation, isolation, addictions, depression, financial distress, and low self-esteem. She has shown remarkable courage to survive at all. However, if her story resembles a soap opera, at least it has occasional excitement and diversion. Our next straight spouse experiences less obvious pain but knows the torture of languishing on a frustrating plateau.

PARALYZED: "ISOLATED AND STUCK"

Matt and Sharon met at their workplace, where they were both mental health professionals. They had an idyllic beginning. During those first years together, Matt *thought it was as close to perfect as a marriage could get.* Matt's father had died when the boy was only six, and his mother remarried, then divorced his stepfather when Matt was a teenager. He had felt huge loss over these events and had longed for a secure, peaceful home of his own.

Both in their late thirties, Matt and Sharon were anxious to start a family and eagerly awaited the birth of their first child. They doted on Danny from the moment he was born. Matt was determined to give his son the perfect childhood he had missed, and Sharon was his partner in it all. *I received unconditional positive regard, as both a husband and a father, from my former wife. We were friends as well as mates and collaborated on all important life decisions.* Matt defined and validated his life primarily as husband and father, rather than through his career. His family was the center of his world.

But that world crashed on August 11, 1995. Sharon called Matt at work to say that she had something important to talk about that evening. *Basically, she just came out and said, "You need to know I love you, but I'm gay."* Her coming out was totally abrupt. There were no obvious clues in the six years before, though she had undergone therapy "to deal with old family issues," and she did have several gay friends. Utterly shocked, Matt felt a flash of fury and had a momentary thought that he wanted to strangle this woman who was destroying their family. His desperate thoughts passed quickly and he sank into deep grief over his stunning loss.

Matt was the first to know about Sharon's lesbian identity. He immediately phoned his close relatives to break the news, and then Sharon flew to Florida to tell her family. She carried with her a letter from Matt, expressing his sadness, but also his understanding and support. To that point, she had not acted on her homosexual identity.

The days that followed were horrible for Matt. *The only thing I can compare it to was when my mother died.* Indeed, this was yet another death to be grieved—that of their relationship that had seemed so right. It was also the death of the Sharon he thought he knew. While Matt was struggling to adjust, cycling from periods of denial to depression, to anger, to glimmers of acceptance, Sharon rapidly changed her appearance *to reflect a more stereotypical lesbian look. She cut off her hair and dressed more "manly."* At first Matt thought she might be bisexual, and he urged her to consider this possibility to save their marriage. But Sharon was adamant about her self-identity as a lesbian. Within a few weeks Matt didn't resist her changes. He says, *In a way, it helped me accept the reality of the situation sooner.* Sadly, he settled into a pattern of accommodation.

Matt went through many predictable stages of grief in the next months, trying to assimilate what was happening and keep some sense of balance. The intensity of his determination to protect his four-year-old son led to an unusual strategy. Matt moved into the spare bedroom within a few weeks, but he and Sharon both stayed in their home. This living arrangement continued for a year prior to their divorce and for two years afterward! Despite their obvious stress during and after the divorce, they made it work, *living amicably as friends.*

It was a strain! Always, Danny's welfare was foremost. After three years in this difficult situation, Sharon wanted a change. She'd settled on a lesbian mate and wanted privacy. Following his pattern of adjustment and self-sacrifice, Matt moved out of their home and let Sharon stay there with her new partner. An equal-time co-parenting arrangement was determined, with Danny spending one week with Matt and the next with Sharon. Matt rented an apartment nearby and did his best to make it comfortable and inviting. Little Danny—precocious, personable, and sensitive—seemed to adjust.

Despite Matt's generosity regarding the house and financial support, Sharon's attitudes abruptly turned negative. Before, she'd said that she loved him *as much as she could any man.* Now suddenly she expressed only coldness. Matt puzzled, *I can't do anything to please her. Everything is filtered through her anger.* Why her fury? Jealousy over Danny? Fear of losing him to Matt? Guilt? Sharon's hostility was Matt's most painful wound of all.

Fast-forward five years and the story is the same. The living arrangements haven't changed and neither have the attitudes of the people. Matt still feels betrayed. His voice is flat and he says he has *no zest for this bipolar life. One week I'm a parent, and the next week, nothing.* He has no network, no new relationship, and no incentive to take care of himself. Weekends, he goes to films, browses bookstores, and cleans house on Sunday to prepare his home for Danny's return. He's filled with sorrow over his ongoing conflict with Sharon and constantly gives in to avoid fights. She rebuffs even his attempts at friendship now.

And he is anxious. Will his job funding be cut? How will he pay the bills when he's already struggling as the only wage earner? He worries about the world situation and about how Danny will face the issues of puberty and middle school teasing. Matt's health is also a concern. Over fifty now, with considerable weight gain, he feels bad about his appearance but doesn't have the energy to exercise or take care of himself. *I don't think Danny has seen me at my best,* he says sadly.

Matt seems groundless. He has searched for comfort in spiritual readings and says, *I'm envious of people of faith.* An agnostic of Jewish heritage, his present interest lies in Eastern philosophy, but he has found no answers. He characterizes his state as *existential angst. I can't let go yet and give my life to a higher power. I've got to do more to create my own joy.* Matt sincerely wants to be happy but can't seem to make it happen. *My intention is to make life good. I've approached this situation with humanity and kindness. There is no reason to be angry. I don't want to spend the rest of my life in resentment.* Childhood losses, not fully grieved, are making his adult loss harder, and his recent emotional suppression has made his pain linger. In the meantime, he has tried psychotherapy and medication to overcome his depression, and he concludes that he needs more courage to make a change.

Lonely and isolated, Matt is a long way from emotional recovery. He lives in limbo. Yet he seems resigned to repeat his patterns with no change, at least until Danny is out of school. Matt has put his own life on hold.

The regretful stories of Kim and Matt exemplify some of the dangers and emotional darkness of many straight spouses. But not everyone is a victim and not everyone gets stuck in a negative outcome. Our third story encourages hope.

A THRIVING EXEMPLAR: "MOVING ON"

Bonnie's marriage lasted for twenty-eight years. For the first fourteen years, she and Stan had an "ideal" marriage based on trust and the innocence of idealistic youngsters married in the early 1960s. They enjoyed being together and had a mutually satisfying sex life. Their three young sons were a joy. Bonnie remembers that in those early years, *Life was meaningful and challenging and rewarding as we encouraged and delighted in each other.*

Then their lives upended. Stan was teaching in his elementary school classroom on a weekday morning, when Bonnie read a letter he had left at home. It was written to his gay lover. Her first reaction was disbelief. Just the thought that her husband had engaged in a homosexual encounter was totally beyond her experience: *I didn't know our friend was gay. Then, I didn't recognize anyone who was gay. I didn't even know the words homophobia or gay or bisexual! I was a college graduate, but I felt very unlearned.* Utterly shocked by her discovery, she had received no warning of the changes that were imminent.

Bonnie somehow got through that terrible day. *I couldn't wait until he came home and we could talk. Our sons were in the backyard playing and my husband and I had a "visit"!* After their confrontation over the letter, Bonnie *felt sick—in her whole being*. After a few days, she grew worse.

I'd been unable to sleep or eat, and had terrible headaches. I'd take two aspirin, not knowing I was allergic to them, and drink them down with coffee—no thought of food! Four hours later, I'd take two more aspirin. When I was vomiting blood, I called the school and Stan rushed me to the hospital.

At 2:00 a.m., two days later, Bonnie underwent emergency surgery. The doctors couldn't stop the bleeding. It took eight pints of blood to save her life. Stan was deeply shaken and felt totally responsible for her plight. When Bonnie finally returned home after ten days in the hospital, Stan did everything possible to make it right. Though he had experimented with homosexual encounters, he and Bonnie still had great affection for each other and a sense of responsibility to their three little boys, just fourteen months, three years, and six years old at the time.

A significant opportunity emerged at this critical moment. A couples' class was forming at their church. Six couples agreed to meet six times in a Sunday evening study group facilitated by the minister and his wife. Stan and Bonnie joined, hoping to find a way to heal and maintain their marriage. The class coalesced. A college professor, engineer, teachers, a librarian, and others found that they had much in common. At the end of six sessions, the group didn't want to disband, so it continued into the next month and the next. Fifteen years later, they were still meeting regularly and giving friendly support to one another. Bonnie says, *That group changed our lives! It was a meaningful experience that enabled each couple to see that what they felt wasn't unique, but shared by the group. It clearly improved our marriage and gave us many more years together. I was happy; he was happy.*

They kept their marriage intact partly through the encouragement of these friends (who were unaware of Stan's bisexuality), and partly through their private agreement. *We decided that we wanted to be married and we wanted to be married to each other. However, if he ever wanted to relate to a man, he had to be honest with himself and with me and we would decide what to do at that time.*

Bonnie was convinced that she couldn't change Stan's sexual orientation or behavior. *For as long as my husband chose to be married, it couldn't have been a better marriage. We enjoyed being together.*

Though bisexual, Stan *chose not to act on that dimension of his life.* Their agreement was that they would be faithful to each other as long as they chose to stay married. However, if Stan acted on his homosexuality, that would end their marriage.

Ten years after Bonnie discovered Stan's sexual orientation, they began family counseling to work primarily with one son, who was having trouble communicating and relating and following the household rules. As the couple continued to meet with their counselor, Stan shared his fear of feeling attracted to men but again declared his intention not to pursue this attraction. Again, the two made a conscious decision to remain married. This agreement, honored in good faith by both partners, allowed them to have another fifteen years as a couple.

But time ran out on their agreement. Bonnie hit her lowest point one late autumn afternoon, one month before their twenty-eighth anniversary. She met Stan in the park to sort out family problems. Sitting on a park bench in the quiet of fall, they talked of their grown children, all of whom were in some state of transition. One was finishing a U.S. Navy hitch and returning from active duty in Desert Storm; another was planning his wedding after spring graduation from college; the third was job-hunting, just out of the army and on medical disability. Everyone in the family was already stressed. Bonnie feared that any added trouble would burden the whole family beyond endurance. But Stan's resolve had weakened. He had met his man. Bonnie's dilemma was clear: Stan had a male soul mate, *and I would no longer be a wife—his wife. That's all I ever wanted to be.*

Nine more months passed after that day in the park before they reached the brink of final separation. *We came home from church one Sunday morning and my husband sat on our bed with hands holding his head and said, "I can't do this any longer!"* That was it. Bonnie was firm. *Then it's time for us to separate. I'm moving.* Bonnie had already made her plan. *My turning point was deciding to do what all of the experts suggest one not do—move, change jobs, find new friends, start over.*

Before they separated, however, Bonnie and Stan agreed that they would tell their whole story to their family and closest friends. It was important to open up this secret they had shared only with each other for nearly three decades so that loved ones could understand their separation. Together, they devised their method. First, they each composed letters, explaining their reasons for this sudden separation.

They gathered the family and read their letters aloud. After they answered everyone's questions, they left their stunned "audience" alone, so their loved ones could talk to and help one another recover. After breaking the news to their family, they repeated the process with a group of their closest friends.

In the meantime, Bonnie prepared to move away. She took only four weekends to gather her things, tie up details, and pack her little U-Haul. *It all came together. I knew, inside my soul, it was the right thing to be doing. Our whole family was present as I drove down the street.* Even at their moment of separation, the family held together—though changed. Bonnie remembers her children's concern. *My youngest son said, "Mom, you can't drive and cry at the same time, so make sure you pull over to the side of the road." My husband had to pick up the pieces with them. They did it together. I was there in their thoughts.*

Bonnie did start over. Making a new home in Lincoln, she moved forward with her own life in an amazingly positive way. She took a job as a sorority housemother at a private Methodist university and enrolled in a master's program. She again became active in a church. Later, she taught in a junior college and enjoyed cultural, musical, theatrical, and spiritual events on the campus, developing friendships along the way. She also took care of her health, starting a regular exercise program and keeping her weight in check.

It wasn't easy! Remember that this plucky woman was grieving the loss of a twenty-eight-year marriage and missing all the comforts and security of her supportive family nearby. She was alone now, frustrated by the lack of resources available for people like her, whose mixed-orientation marriages crashed. She sought professional counseling and a general women's support group, but her best comfort came from confiding in close friends and family members—her sister, niece, her sons, and old friends in California.

In times of confusion and doubt, Bonnie longed to read about how other couples worked through such pain, but there were precious few books on the subject and no support groups in her town. At times she felt very angry. She often felt that Stan had ruined their marriage, had disrupted the lives of their sons and their families. Bonnie no longer had the companionship and love of a husband or the luxuries of her old home. Her dream of growing old together with Stan was crushed. Their plan to travel and write children's history books after retirement was now impossible. It was terribly depressing at times. Bonnie had to rely on her own inner resources through much of her recovery. Her natural optimism and faith helped, along with her practical, hard-working nature. Because she's also compassionate, she wanted to make recovery easier for others, so she helped to start Lincoln's Straight Spouse Network support group, working with the area's PFLAG (Parents, Families and Friends of Lesbians and Gays) chapter. She acted as facilitator for six years, until she finished her master's degree and moved to another state to teach college-level classes at a technology institute.

Once again, Bonnie established herself in a new community. As a teacher and sorority housemother, she enjoyed campus and church activities. Achieving her master's degree and starting her new professional career enhanced her self-esteem immensely. Now, encouraged by an editor, she has published her master's thesis as a book. She is a role model for overcoming challenges and re-creating oneself.

Perhaps Bonnie's best news is that she is no longer lonely. Nearly nine eventful years after she and Stan parted, she has remarried. Gloriously happy now, she describes her new husband as *spiritual, intellectual, thoughtful, romantic, gray-haired handsome, sexy, fun, and caring. This intimate experience is absolutely what I have been searching for throughout my life, sensing the whole person—body, mind, and spirit!* Bonnie has triumphed. She's managed to move through her fears and tears and painful growth to create a rewarding new life.

If all straight spouses could have a happy outcome like Bonnie's, there would be no need for this book. But not everyone fares so well. Again, many confusing variables exacerbate the mixed-orientation experience. Natural tendencies, basic view of life, financial resources, education, access to counseling, family closeness, support of friends, spiritual grounding, health, self-image, and countless other factors affect coping ability. These and other influences on later happiness will be examined in other chapters, as we try to discern key contributors to thriving after crisis.

PREPARATION FOR THIS COURSE IN RECOVERY

After each chapter of this book, you will be asked to ponder key questions and write in a journal your impressions, feelings, and responses. This is a critical element in your healing. It will be a dialogue between you and the real people on the pages of this textbook for recovery.

Keeping a journal is a very private activity, not an academic exercise. It is meant for your personal use, to be shared only when you choose, or not at all. Therefore, it should contain only absolutely authentic, honest answers to the questions posed, expanded by any other ideas or thoughts that come to you at the time. Your journal belongs only to you, so you can turn off your inner critic and just write. The activity is a valuable tool to record your growth and evolution into wholeness. Later, you may look back and be proud of healthy progress.

QUESTIONS TO PONDER

1. Is your pattern as a straight spouse similar to Kim's or Matt's or Bonnie's?
2. If you recognize yourself in one of these histories, is there something you'd like to change about your own response?
3. What clues can you discern in these three stories for more constructive action?

ACTIVITY

Purchase a new spiral-bound notebook for your journal. Use it only for this purpose, and write in it after reading each chapter—or as often as you feel the urge to express your thoughts. "Questions to Ponder" will get you started. Write your own story as you progress through this book. Start with your answers to the previous questions: How are you like the people you've just read about? How is your situation different? Your journal can offer insights and eventually guidance on your unique path of healing. Write honestly and spontaneously for your most important audience: YOU.

Chapter 2

Coming Out Three Ways

Coming out is an intensely individual process, particularly difficult if a gay person is intimately partnered with a heterosexual mate. This chapter examines three common scenarios where a straight spouse is involved. Some gays choose to stay married, using that public image as a cover for a double life. Others decide to leave their heterosexual relationship shortly after they acknowledge their own homosexuality. Another less common choice is the endless closet, in which the couple lives together with their secret intact.

Often it takes many years to come to terms with the fact of one's homosexuality. Fear of rejection or retribution or even physical safety is daunting, causing gays to delay facing reality. But their gradual realization leads eventually to a crisis of authenticity. In the meantime, gays may pursue heterosexual relationships and choose to marry, attempting to avoid acknowledging their natural sexual identity. Some think that they'll "get over it" by marrying. Painful self-doubt is often layered with feelings of guilt. Only after they pass a critical point can they admit, even to themselves, that they are indeed homosexual. While this internal struggle simmers or rages, often for decades, the straight mate may be blissfully unaware of impending crisis. This was certainly the case in Carol Grever's marriage to Jim. Here is her first-person account.

LIVING THE DOUBLE LIFE

Jim and I were very young and inexperienced when we married in the early 1960s. We'd grown up in the innocent Eisenhower era of family idealization, illustrated in television sitcoms like Father Knows Best *and* Leave It to Beaver. *Watching June Cleaver bake*

When Your Spouse Comes Out
Published by The Haworth Press, Taylor & Francis Group, 2008. All rights reserved.
doi:10.1300/6046_02

cookies in her spotless televised kitchen didn't suggest what was really in store. Reared in a sheltered, conservative home, I knew nothing of homosexuality at that time, and Jim wasn't much better informed. We met at the church youth group, were high school sweethearts, and were both virgins when we married in college. Jim had been my only serious boyfriend.

We'd been married for several years before Jim came to terms with his own sexuality. By then, we had a young son. In a recent letter to a college friend, he recalled his experience in those early years and sent me a copy of his thoughts. He wanted me to understand why he acted as he did.

> I didn't realize that I was gay until I was married and had a kid (I was about age twenty-four). Looking back, I definitely had earlier clues about my sexuality but didn't have the background or experience to read them. My first reaction to this realization was guilt, thanks to religion, especially since I was working for the church in Oregon at the time. I was able to overcome the guilt with the insight that I did not choose homosexuality, that I was made that way. And if I believed that God made me and that God doesn't make mistakes, then I was not a mistake.
>
> Since I had made my bed (marriage and fatherhood), I decided the best thing to do was to lie in it. So I continued in my marriage and family for the next thirty years. During that time I had many sexual encounters, mostly anonymous, with other men. My homosexual drive was a hunger that I could either feed and it would go away for awhile—a few days, weeks, maybe months—or I could deny it and it would consume my consciousness. I rationalized that it was better to feed it and it would abate . . . and I could get on with the job of being husband, father, businessman, etc. I also rationalized that I was not being unfaithful because (1) there was no wavering in my marital commitment and (2) my liaisons were with men rather than women. I had no desire to be a part of what I understood to be the "gay lifestyle."

Of course, while Jim was living this compartmentalized existence, I was totally unaware of his extramarital adventures. His decision to "lie" in the bed he had made certainly had double meaning. His guilt over his deception was assuaged by his rationalization that he was "faithful" to me because his sexual encounters were homosexual, not with other women. He lived this way for three decades, with more than 1,000 anonymous sexual partners. He might have continued this secret double life unendingly had he not fallen in love. In his letter to his college roommate, Jim continued his story.

In 1990, I met a man that I fell in love with. Prior to that, my homosexual activities were based solely on lust. I discovered with him that it was possible to passionately and romantically love another man. About this time, Carol's dad was dying and she was in a pretty bad place. And I was beginning to see that there could be an alternate life out there for me—but scared shitless to embrace it. So we were having some marital difficulties and were discussing a trial separation. Despite the fact that a trial separation could have given me the opportunity to explore that alternate life, I was in utmost anguish regarding leaving the life I had lived for so long.

Like Stan, in the previous chapter, Jim kept his stake in our marriage until midlife, when he became emotionally attached to another man. This attraction was markedly different from the anonymous encounters he'd used to satisfy sexual need previously. Now he faced a true dilemma.

In this deep anguish, I confessed to Carol my "homosexual tendencies." I had not intended to tell her. It was just like someone else was controlling my tongue. I really feel that God intervened directly in my life at this point. I had expected Carol to be livid, telling me that I had taken the best years of her life, yada, yada—but she was very sympathetic, saying, "You poor dear, having to carry such a tremendous secret all these years." I really felt the weight of the world lifted from my shoulders with that revelation to her. I told her that I would stay with her as long as it was beneficial to her. What I didn't realize is that I transferred at least a part of my burden to her.

Jim had gone over the edge in telling me about his homosexuality. His coming out surprised us both, since he hadn't really planned it. The strain of my dad's last illness, flying back and forth to Tulsa from Boulder when he was worse, juggling demands of our business, keeping up appearances in my highly visible profession, and Jim's increasing distance had worn me down. I felt completely unsupported in Jim's coldness, and facing the loss of my beloved father felt like my own death. That spring, I had suggested our separation to sort things out and Jim had been looking for another place to live, at least temporarily.

On the Friday before Memorial Day, 1991, he left to sign a lease on a rental he'd found. I went into my flower garden to find solace from the layers of grief over the threatened loss of these two dearest men of my life. When Jim came through the gate and walked toward me, his face was ashen. We sat down on the retaining wall as the sun slipped behind the mountain. He said slowly, "I just couldn't do it. I couldn't sign the lease." His fear of being alone had stopped him from making the break. After a long pause, he finally let go and gave me the seed of the truth he'd hidden for so many years. But he gave me only the edge of the whole story: "I have homosexual tendencies." It was only in the ensuing months and years that I learned more of his hidden history—one I'll never know completely.

Jim's spontaneous confession answered so many nagging questions for me—his habitual emotional distance, frequent trips alone, his sudden interest in fund-raising for the local AIDS project, changes in his appearance, his cultivation of friends I didn't know. Now it all made sense. The burden he transferred to me that day was self-doubt, confusion, and the conviction that I was utterly stupid for not suspecting his homosexuality. Yet I didn't feel angry at the time, only sympathetic that his fear had forced him to hide his true self for so long. Ever the nurturer, I tried to comfort him as he wept in my arms. At the moment he came out, I felt strangely calm—or perhaps numb. It was only later that we dealt with the implications and damage of his thirty years of duplicity.

It is significant that Jim intended to stay married to me: he could have had it both ways—homosexual enjoyment under cover of a conventional marriage. He feared the sea change of divorce and venturing into a totally different life.

Jim's desire to remain in the marriage reveals an apparent gender difference in gay behavior. Some gay men successfully compartmentalize their activities and their feelings, as Jim did for decades. Practically speaking, men can use marriage as a cover for clandestine casual sex with other men. They go out, have a brief, often anonymous sexual encounter, then return home and put the one-hour stand behind them. Lesbians, on the other hand, appear to have more difficulty with the partitioned life and tend to leave their marriages when they clearly understand and accept their homosexual identity. This difference in approach is exemplified in the next case study.

A FASTER TRACK

Kit's story illustrates the tendency to break more cleanly from marriage into a clearly same-sex lifestyle once homosexual orientation is acknowledged. Like Sharon, described previously, Kit also came to her sexual self-identification after several years of experimentation and denial, though she loved Phil and had married him with a conscious desire to have children. Phil remembers their story this way.

I was madly in love and hadn't a clue what "homosexual" was all about, growing up in Cheyenne, Wyoming. Kit was a bit more . . . calculating, which I knew from the start. Though she was also madly in love with me—and she's one of the lesbians who likes men better than women, as friends, even now. She was also after my genes, which she made no bones about: she wanted kids, MY kids. (I was class valedictorian, and she has this thing for academic smarts.)

As it came out much, much later, it also was a denial/social/religious thing, as well. Being one of those <u>lesbians</u> was such a horrid concept to her as a young woman that she did a nice number on herself, burying it. She married me in part to prove to herself that she <u>wasn't</u> a lesbian, as she admitted at one point.

Kit's journey toward self-recognition also took several years, though her sexual orientation was disguised at first, even to herself. She spent years acting out her sexual dissatisfaction through numerous brief affairs with men, rather than women. When she finally acknowledged that it was women who attracted her, her lesbian affairs became more problematic. Her liaisons with women lasted longer and had deeper emotional impact. Phil remembers it as a chaotic time.

Marital troubles started within the first year of marriage. She kept having compulsive affairs with other men. It's hard for me to fathom, now, why I stayed, especially given some of the incentives I had toward the end of that first year. I did love her, of course, and I was stubborn and had made a marriage vow. Maybe it was a bit of karmic debt. We were in counseling, on and off, from our second year of marriage onward, but we were also in the midst of growing up, going to graduate school, finding work, and playing house. Once children were in the picture, I felt obligated to fulfill my husbandly and fatherly duties.

In retrospect, Phil realizes that Kit was as confused as he. Thirteen or fourteen years into their marriage, Kit began to broach the subject of her lesbian tendencies. *She wondered if she might (just maybe, perhaps, possibly, do you suppose) be a little bit bisexual?* Phil contends that Kit's being bisexual was actually not a problem for him. *If anything, it was a bit of a turn-on. . . . I would occasionally joke with her about bringing someone home to share, and I was actually quite open to the possibility, though she never did.* Another couple of years passed before Kit came out fully as a lesbian.

The actual confluence of our decisions at the very end was funny. We had been through a couple of abstinent periods, at Kit's request, and while we had an officially "open" marriage, I hadn't had other partners—I didn't really have the nerve. At the same time, I was do-ing a lot of reading on Tantra and the energy of sex. When Kit and I fi-nally resumed sexual relations after a long period of celibacy, it felt to me like connecting myself to a battery—but backwards. I recall hav-ing sex with Kit only three times in the last six months of our mar-riage, and the last time we had sex together drained me so badly, I had to call in sick to work and spend the weekend recovering.

This was the very weekend Kit left on a cruise with her mother and sister, during which she met her current partner. When she came back, we both had this awkward look about us, and burst out at nearly the same moment, "'We need to talk!'" We went out to a local microbrewery, got a couple of substantial pints, and I told her, "Don't take this wrong, but I don't ever want to have sex with you again." And she said, "Don't take this wrong, but I don't ever want to have sex with you again, either." Well—that wasn't so bad! With that out of the way, we loosened up, then she told me she'd "met someone" and I knew (mostly relieved) that it was time for me to move on. From there, it was just details.

We celebrated our final, seventeenth, anniversary by going out on the town, having a fine meal, quite a bit too much to drink, and spend-ing the evening at a strip joint—her first visit to such a place. It seemed somehow appropriate, and we both had a really good time. The divorce was amicable, no lawyers.

While Kit had married in part to prove to herself that she was not a lesbian, the nagging fact of her basic homosexuality continued to present itself. She could suppress it for periods of time, but it didn't go away. Similarly, Jim's need would build until he acted on it through many years of anonymous sexual encounters.

Cynthia is yet another example. She remembers feeling "different" as early as four or five years old: *Something didn't fit.* She recounted her surreptitious homosexual tendencies during her teen years. Her favorite high school fun was always with girls. She especially liked practicing dance steps together, though the words of Johnny Mathis's songs didn't quite fit her feelings. She remembers swaying with the music, holding a girlfriend, *and I always liked to lead.* Even at that young age, Cynthia always saw herself eventually being a mother, but never a wife.

Cynthia lost her virginity at seventeen to a student teacher, traveled to Europe when she was twenty-two, and experimented further. But she continued to repress her homosexual tendencies and eventually married because she truly wanted children. After her marriage, her homosexual impulses simmered under the surface. Though she loved her husband, she was still attracted to women. Her first real love for a straight woman was followed by a series of lesbian affairs.

Cynthia recalls an epiphany as she sat with her husband in a movie theater and felt an "electric shock" watching two women make love on the screen. She was so shaken that she felt certain everyone around her noticed. She couldn't continue to deny her own sexual identity. She realized that her denial had put her into the closet while she hid behind a strong male. Eventually, Cynthia divorced her husband, moved to another state, and carried on her later life as a lesbian. Committed to personal growth, she admits that she *can't stay in any stagnant situation.* This seems a typical pattern illustrated also by Kit and Sharon. Once these three women faced the power of their sexual identification, they had to pull out of their marriages in order to live authentically.

ENDLESS CLOSET

A clean break may be less painful in the long run than the secret suffering of an endless closet. While no conclusive data exist, anecdotal evidence indicates that one-third of all mixed-orientation couples attempt to stay together, and half of those (approximately 15 percent) actually do so for three or more years (PFLAG, 2006). Those who remain in the relationship do so for a variety of reasons, often to protect the children, or for economic or religious or appearance considerations. For some, their love for each other overcomes the homosexual challenge and they maintain a deep and lasting bond. In those rare cases, there is enough genuine affection, respect, and history to make the effort seem worthwhile. Other couples who stay together are motivated by fear. To these gays who remain married to a straight spouse, it seems better to live with the familiar pain of duplicity or repression, rather than risk something worse, as Jim pointed out.

Kaye and Joseph exemplify this decision. Married for more than forty years, Kaye has been aware of Joseph's homosexuality for thirty of those years. Their marriage has survived numerous crises, which Kaye describes as *a roller-coaster ride—ranging from despair to joy.* Joseph's first disclosure came early in their marriage, when their two children were very young.

He told me on a walk one evening. It seems like it came out of the blue. I don't remember a preamble. He just said he'd begun to realize he wasn't like some men when it came to sex—that he looked at it differently. He said he didn't think I understood that he was bisexual. Joseph then told his wife of his first homosexual encounter with her cousin. At that time, it was his only gay experience.

Kaye accepted her husband's confession with equanimity and understanding. She received it as an isolated incident. But several years later, he revealed *an established relationship and a history of occasional (perhaps even frequent) casual encounters.* That second unveiling *was much more traumatic.*

Yet Kaye and Joseph determinedly stayed together, rearing their two children, pursuing successful academic careers, and working through their crises. It has been hard! Kaye has endured periods of emotional isolation and deep loneliness. Still, both people remain steadfast. Kaye says, *We love each other very much and are committed to each other. We treasure the ongoingness of our marriage and family. Our relationship hasn't been as emotionally intense and close as it once was. I miss our sexual intimacy—even though it had its difficulties—but I can live with its absence. It's emotional distance and disconnection that I can't bear.*

Kaye's endurance of her ambivalent situation has taken its toll on her emotions and her health. She suffers debilitating arthritis and periodic depression. She also experiences recurring anxiety episodes. Ties with her two grown children are strained by their anger and confusion over Joseph's coming out to the family. Wiser from her difficulties, Kaye advises anyone who remains in the closet with a gay spouse to *get a good therapist—and be as true to oneself and one's husband as possible. Whatever comes out of that is most likely to be right.* Now retired from their professional responsibilities, enjoying prosperity and improved relations with their children and grandchildren, Kaye and Joseph both seem resigned to their endless closet.

The couples described in this chapter illustrate three additional common patterns of behavior in mixed-orientation relationships—the double life, the quick split, and the endless closet. They demonstrate typical but contrasting decisions among couples that affect their long-term outcome. However it is handled, the personal challenges for everyone involved when a mate comes out mark the beginning of a long, arduous process of recovery. Considerable research has been done on straight spouses' responses. A textbook example follows in the next chapter.

QUESTIONS TO PONDER

1. Given your own mixed-orientation dilemma, try to picture yourself in the happiest, healthiest situation possible. Dream a little! Imagine your ideal outcome in vivid detail. Envision yourself in that best-case scene. Can you think of a first step toward that dream?
2. Three patterns of behavior are illustrated in this chapter: double life, quick split, endless closet. Can you discern possible motivations or causal factors behind each?

ACTIVITIES

1. Write in your journal a description of your imagined ideal outcome. Try to "see" it and feel it in living color and exquisite detail.
2. Check the local availability of a straight spouse support group. Look for PFLAG in the phone book and check the PFLAG and SSN (Straight Spouse Network) Web sites for more resources and information: www.pflag.org and www.straightspouse.org. Visit a support group meeting, if possible.

Chapter 3

Steps Toward Resolution:
A Typical Example

There is a fairly predictable pattern of reactions to the discovery that one's mate is homosexual. Self-reports of more than 2,000 straight and gay spouses were summarized in the publication *Opening the Straight Spouse's Closet* (PFLAG, 1994).

Typically, the first reaction is shock at the unsuspected news that one's intimate partner has a different sexual orientation from your own. There is usually an odd sense of relief, however, when many unexplained details of the relationship become clear. It is the "Ah, then it isn't me!" reaction. Confusion is common, followed by denial of the reality of the situation. Most people experience some self-blame: "What could I have done to prevent this? Is it my fault that he's gay?" In some cases, there is heart-felt sympathy for the anguish of the gay partner. All these early reactions occur repeatedly, not necessarily in order, with incredible intensity.

Sooner or later, straight spouses realize that there is no turning back. They face their new reality squarely. Stark awareness ushers in anger, grief, and despair. This dangerous but necessary phase takes months or years to resolve. Grief must be endured—over the betrayal of trust, the loss of love, and the obliteration of future plans. When straight spouses recognize the implications of their loss and the ominous risk to their health and future, their anger can deepen to rage. Those who get stuck in their anger never really heal. Burdened by the sheer weight of conflicting emotions, many of these wounded people experience periods of utter despair. They feel hopeless. Individuals move into and out of all these typical stages, usually repeatedly, often without warning at surprising moments. A relatively good day can

When Your Spouse Comes Out
Published by The Haworth Press, Taylor & Francis Group, 2008. All rights reserved.
doi:10.1300/6046_03

descend into the black hole of despair, sometimes with no apparent trigger.

Eventually, most straight spouses experience a turning point, finding enough inner strength to begin healing. This usually happens when they accept that which they cannot change. They progress into the future, rather than remaining stuck in the past. Only then can anger be replaced by forgiveness, or at least by movement toward resolution. Only then can trust and hope be restored. Straight spouses who rely on their own inner resources, reinforced by some belief or meaning beyond themselves, seem to fare best. The strongest, or most fortunate, build a new life, wiser after their ordeal. This is true resolution, and they move into the next phase of their lives.

This is a skeletal outline of what one might expect after a mate comes out. Details are examined from various angles throughout the book, but it is useful to keep this overview in mind (see Figure 3.1). Though research on this sequence of experience was initially based on testimony of men and women in similar English-speaking cultures—the United States, Canada, England, and Australia—the pattern appears in other countries as well. The straight spouse experience is multicultural and knows no geographic boundaries.

This chapter will demonstrate these recognized stages of recovery through a closer look at one who experienced the whole sequence. Meet Zhi Wen, a forty-four-year-old woman of Chinese descent. She was born in Indonesia and educated in Chinese schools in Thailand and Malaysia. Later, Zhi traveled to North America as a college student. After earning two university degrees in Canada, she stayed on as a skilled immigrant. She later became a naturalized Canadian citizen. Despite her multinational background, her basic story might

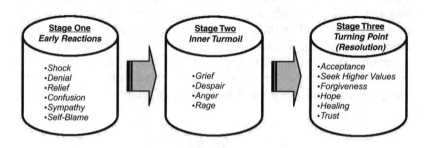

FIGURE 3.1. Straight Mate Recovery Stages

have been told by an American or an Australian or a South African, or by a straight spouse in almost any country.

EARLY REACTIONS

As a bright twenty-one-year-old student, Zhi was eager to leave Asia and come to a new world. She had studied in private boarding schools in Thailand and Malaysia up to that point. In the West, she hoped for more respect than she'd found as a Chinese girl living outside China.

Zhi did well in her studies, completing one undergraduate degree, then returning to Canada two years later to enroll in a second bachelor of arts program. This time, she had an added benefit—a warm, family environment where she boarded. She developed a real kinship with the couple who owned the home where she rented space. By the time she finished her studies, she felt like a daughter to them. *Since these close friends treated me much better than my own parents (I did not grow up with my parents, anyway), they became my godparents,* she recalled fondly.

Zhi met Tom, her American mate, at her place of work. At first, Tom seemed very committed to Zhi. As they grew closer, she trusted him completely and traveled often to be with him when he moved back and forth between Canada and the United States. She suspected nothing specific, though she says, *Somehow, I knew something was not right, but I also blamed myself for not doing enough.* The two managed to stay together for seven years.

On April 6, 2001, Zhi's trust was crushed. Opening a letter from Tom, she was confounded by his abrupt confession of homosexuality. It was a long letter, but the burning point was that Tom is gay. *Seven years in relationship, bit by bit, I knew at least something about him . . . but not the gay part! I cried for an hour after I read the letter. Then I phoned my cousin (the closest friend I have). She was in disbelief. I said I had to talk, so we met in a restaurant. My cousin had no idea what to do with me. She just sat with me. I finally went home around 10:00.*

That night, I couldn't sleep at all. I cried hysterically. At times, I found difficulty breathing. Perhaps I cried too much. I managed to phone the 1-800 crisis line and got somebody on the line and talked. I didn't know what to do next. I didn't even know whether I should drink a sip of water. The lady on the phone instructed me to take some milk every two hours. My mouth particularly was affected. The jaw locked up and I couldn't eat any solid food for thirteen days. All I could take was a little milk.

Zhi's immediate response to her mate's confession is not surprising. A shock of this magnitude obviously destroys every assumption about the relationship. The earth seems to shift to a crazy angle. This disorientation is the first stage, followed closely by utter confusion.

Zhi struggled to understand her new situation. *On the third day, I could not cope with my pain anymore. I phoned my godmother in Winnipeg. She was more than a mother to me. I consulted her on every major thing in my life and she was very dear to me!* Zhi was fortunate to have a confidante with experience. Another surprise came when she learned just how much experience!

My godmother had a similar scenario thirty-nine years ago, before she even knew my godfather. She had never told me about this part of her life. She fell in love with her professor at graduate school. Their relationship was relatively brief, lasting a year and a half, but the professor was married at the time and had two very young children. When he came out to my godmother, she told him that he had to tell his wife. It took that man another three years to confess to his wife. His marriage broke up with a very bitter divorce and a big fight for custody. Still, after his divorce, the man turned to my godmother as a listener and they have remained good friends since then.

Zhi's godmother urged her to forgive Tom, insisting that they could remain friends. But it was too soon even to suggest that. Zhi said, *I was so confused. I didn't know what I should do next, but I did know one thing—my belief system had collapsed and was totally bankrupt.* Though she couldn't follow her godmother's well-intentioned advice, Zhi felt fortunate to have a loving, understanding listener she could trust.

Zhi's vague fear that she was somehow responsible for the breakup was soon dispelled. As Tom's story unfolded, she learned that he had been openly gay before they met. He had previously had a three-year affair with another man, even following him to Italy where they had lived together. Zhi's earlier doubts about "not doing enough" in their relationship turned to relief—at least on that score.

THE NEW REALITY

As days passed, Zhi struggled to understand what was happening. She continued *to dig and dig to put the pieces together.* She was careful not to jump to wrong conclusions. *I confronted him in some major areas to ensure I did not make any wrong judgments about him. For example, I made him admit to me how many relationships that he had in the past. There were a lot of denials on his side, but I did not buy them all.*

Echoing most straight spouses, Zhi still asks herself, *How come I was so blind and so vulnerable? How come I let people use me while I offered my pure heart? How come I was the last to know? Did I ever pay attention to the hints?* Trusting Tom, she was systematically misled by his double life. *With me, he was one person. When I was not there, he would cruise around looking for mates. He had many encounters with different men.* Though she blames herself for not questioning his actions *(Stupid me!)*, she thinks she simply trusted him too much. *He told lies, one after the other. I still find difficulty in believing how a person could lie that much. I will never understand in my life.*

When it was clear to Zhi that Tom had betrayed her trust from the beginning, she was enraged. *I had a lot of violent thoughts. Hire a gang to beat him up. Phone him and scold him to my heart's content. Things like that. At times, those thoughts just drove me crazy. With God's grace I managed not to take any actions, but it was not easy. However, sometimes, particularly the first few months, I felt that my crazy thoughts left me no way out because nobody would understand my feelings.*

Three months after Tom came out to her, Zhi gave up on any thought of reconciliation. *I learned that my mate's partner moved in with him in late July. I called Tom and his partner picked up the phone. When I confronted Tom, he was speechless. This was the last thing he wanted me to know in this whole world. My heart ached.*

Zhi was about to take another serious blow: she would soon lose her closest confidante. *In late September, I learned that my dear godmother was diagnosed with the final stage of lung cancer and she was dying. It was my lowest point. I felt I'd lost all my worldly support.* Life was extremely difficult for Zhi as she traveled frequently to Winnipeg to see her loved one slipping away. *The two most significant people in my life, my mate and my godmother, left me in the space of one year.* Her surrogate mother died on April 15, 2002. Zhi faced the darkest reality of her losses. Her grief turned to despair and she considered suicide.

TURNING POINT

In desperation, Zhi again dialed the Toronto crisis line and was referred to a good counselor she described as *a real angel to me.* Zhi believes she might not have survived the following seven months without therapy. *My struggles were two steps forward and one step backward. At times, it could be four steps forward and five steps backward.* She didn't give up. She read everything she could find about mixed-orientation marriages, learning of PFLAG and SSN. She regularly participated in SSN gatherings. Attending meetings with others on the same journey became her *long-term therapy.* Slowly, Zhi began to feel stronger, approaching acceptance.

Another helper in these dark days was her cat, Mimi. *She was the only one who stayed close physically with me in the loneliest time of my life. She came to lick my tears when I cried. She sat on my lap when I meditated at night.* Sharing their sorrow with a furry friend is common to many straight spouses. Though they can't talk to us, our pets somehow seem to understand and give unconditional love.

Perhaps most important, Zhi clung to her core beliefs. During her therapy, she had refused the counselor's recommendation to take antidepressant drugs, *hoping that God would help me, although my faith was not strong at that time.* A Siddha Yoga practitioner, she follows the teachings of Baba, her guru. *In my toughest time, I turned to my guru. I asked him what I should do because my trust system was totally collapsed. Baba said to me, "Turn within! That is the only thing you can do." I believe that the most important thing I learned is that love is from within. Turning within worked for me. Now the connection to God is most important in every issue in my life.*

RESOLUTION

Finding meaning beyond herself in her spiritual practice, Zhi has found the grace to accept her former mate with equanimity. She describes her current feelings about Tom in this way. *I fully accept gay people as God's creations. Everyone wants to be loved and cared for. I feel sad that Tom cannot be true to himself, but I feel very compassionate toward him. I would just say that I do not understand what he has in his mind. As I wrote to him in my final letter, my pain will become the scar in my life. I will not forget, but I don't have to constantly remember.*

Zhi's history is almost a template of recovery, typical of many others who emerge from a mixed-orientation marriage bloodied but not defeated. She wonders, though, *if human beings only learn when we go through hard times.* Her present physical, mental, and emotional states are generally healthy. Learning to trust a relationship again will be her most difficult task. At times she still feels sad or angry, but she stays with her goal of living a positive life. Her cat, Mimi, has died, but Zhi volunteers as a foster parent for the Humane Society. *I hope to help animals as Mimi helped me and saved my life.*

Meditation and her guru's teachings have been instrumental in Zhi's recovery. She summarizes her present state philosophically: *At a deeper level, I see the whole experience as part of my Karma. I have learned not to pay revenge and have learned how to forgive. I have come closer to my God and my heart. Perhaps it is not that bad.*

QUESTIONS TO PONDER

Review the stages of coping at the beginning of this chapter.

1. Can you identify where you stand today in that process?
2. Have you experienced any, or all, of these stages?
3. Have you repeated any of the stages?
4. Does it help to know that millions of others have felt as you do?

ACTIVITY

After writing your thoughts on these questions in your journal, identify a trusted person to confide in. Share your experience regularly with a relative or friend, or ask for a phone contact of another straight spouse from SSN or PFLAG. Consider group or individual therapy. Talking to an understanding, supportive confidant(e) may help clarify your options.

Part II: Path—Self-Healing Guide
for Straight Spouses

INTRODUCTION TO THE GUIDE

Representative relationships in Part I exhibit typical patterns of straight spouse reactions and create a background for Part II, the *Self-Healing Guide*. This mosaic of individual experience evolves into a map for long-term recovery, suggesting techniques that may also apply to other highly personal crises. The intention is to encourage a proactive process for deep healing that can be used by individuals working alone, with a therapist, or in support groups. In this section, Dr. Deborah Bowman utilizes her expertise as a clinical psychologist to examine and interpret underlying forces in representative case studies.

Chapter 4 contains an introductory explanation of elements of Gestalt theory that are relevant to a straight spouse's challenge. It provides an understandable explanation of some psychological dynamics that impact recovery.

Chapters 5 through 8 present true-life examples to illustrate specific obstacles that often arise when a mixed-orientation relationship ends:

- Immediate personal challenges and risks
- Family and social challenges
- Long-term challenges

Touching stories with professional commentary suggest creative possibilities. Readers struggling with similar situations may thus learn how others recovered from their confusion and moved toward a healthier, happier reality.

Chapter 4

Underlying Psychological Forces

BOUNDARY DISTURBANCES
AND DEFENSE MECHANISMS

When we face strong emotional challenges, it is important to assess our own reactions and coping strategies. Each of us develops unique protections from the "slings and arrows of outrageous fortune." Even as children we learn to buffer or defend ourselves from the pain of difficult environments or negative family situations. These buffers may become habitual defense mechanisms.

As we get older, we continue to use these automatic responses whenever we feel or imagine we are threatened with loss, pain, or fear. We repeat certain defenses, even when they are not appropriate for mature life situations. Recognizing these habitual defensive patterns in our partners helps us understand that their actions are expressions of their own psychological history, not a reflection of our personal worth. Becoming aware of these patterns in ourselves provides us with an opportunity to heal. These habits and survival tools of childhood often prevent awareness of our deep personal needs as adults. Behaviors that were essential earlier in life may now become a hindrance, creating unfinished business that begs for attention.

In this chapter, we will explore five general patterns of defense that were sometimes useful in the past but mostly serve to avoid genuine interpersonal connection in the present (Bowman and Leakey, 2006). When a gay partner comes out and stress is high in the relationship, these five patterns become especially exaggerated and troublesome for both partners. In Gestalt therapy they are called boundary disturbances because they confuse healthy relationships and make genuine contact difficult or impossible (Perls et al., 1951). These boundary

When Your Spouse Comes Out
Published by The Haworth Press, Taylor & Francis Group, 2008. All rights reserved.
doi:10.1300/6046_04

disturbances are introjection, confluence, retroflection, projection, and deflection (Polster and Polster, 1973). Each pattern is defined, discussed, and illustrated in this chapter. Understanding these basic human responses can help straight spouses recognize their own tendencies and begin to change unproductive habits.

INTROJECTION

In the pattern of introjection, we swallow whole information from others without truly choosing or being able to integrate what is offered to us. Imagine children who have been given the message very early that they must earn their parents' love. While this is not a healthy communication of unconditional love, it is one that most individuals are exposed to in the family of origin. When this is the primary introjected message from parents, children internalize the mistaken idea that love can only be earned through their performance in the world. They become habitual "people pleasers."

A person who grows up with this harmful message may cope reasonably well going through life "earning" love through behaviors that are rewarded by others. When the bottom falls out, as in the situation of the straight spouse, this believed thought (introject) is paired with even more devastating messages—I have failed and I do not deserve to be loved. Many common introjects cause difficulty in times of stress. All of them point to messages that essentially devalue our worth and ability to meet our needs.

The larger society adds more of these harmful messages, compounding the sense of loss and failure for someone already suffering pain from childhood conditioning. Often these societal expectations create inner conflict. Such messages include, "I should pretend everything is okay when I'm hurt"; "I should sacrifice my happiness for others"; and "I should have known my partner was gay." The list of possible introjects is inexhaustible. These internalized messages make us feel bad about ourselves.

Most societal introjects compound feelings of shame. Everyone is susceptible to a certain degree of shame in the straight spouse dilemma. No family of origin is perfect or capable of protecting children from all outside influences and shame-based messages. Consider your family of origin. Was it very healthy, mostly healthy, missing important elements, or difficult and primarily painful? Each degree of difference sets up an incrementally maladaptive way of coping with stress and loss.

Individuals with strong negative internal messages experience extreme states of distress. A gay partner's coming out exposes the straight spouse's introject of worthlessness. The old tape of believed thoughts undermines any expectation of a happy marriage. Resulting pain may feel like punishment for the straight spouse's choices and way of being in the world. The example of Kim, in Chapter 1, demonstrates the point. Her present image as victim was predisposed by her early family messages. Today, she says, *I sabotage my own happiness.*

The truth is that almost all straight spouses experience feelings of shame due to unhealthy messages from family and society. This reaction can be expected for varying periods of time. When the response is profound and lingers too long, it usually indicates compounded factors that began earlier in life. These indicators suggest that the crisis could lead to longer-term mental health risks, such as depression, isolation, psychosomatic illness, and addiction. An important self-care step is therefore to recognize and assess the depth of shame and other negative internalized messages.

A key to countering the process of introjection is to identify which messages were assimilated from others without discernment and which ones truly nourished your being. Were you forced to swallow a belief without the opportunity to question or decide whether your values coincided? Do you hold attitudes toward yourself that originated from someone else's negative outlook? These beliefs can originate from parents and then be reinforced during years with a partner whose expressions are similar. It is helpful to identify such negative introjects in your thoughts, speech, and actions. Then gently remind yourself that this is not your essential being but an attitude you assumed when you were not in a position to choose differently.

CONFLUENCE

The next boundary disturbance that can interfere with health and well-being is confluence. This pattern of behavior is defined by merged, confused, enmeshed, and ill-defined boundaries between individuals. When you have difficulty making a distinction between your own fundamental needs and those of another person, you are experiencing confluence. When the pattern is entrenched, you cannot separate your needs from others' or make good contact because you don't know where the other person leaves off and you begin.

Many marriages suffer because this phenomenon is at the core of unstated agreements between partners. This pattern can make differences intolerable to each other, and partners unconsciously agree to give up their individuality and significant interests. It seems likely that this problem is at the core of many of the psychologically compounded difficulties facing straight spouses and their partners. Matt, described in Chapter 1, has subjugated his own needs to those of his ex-wife and son and exemplifies this pattern.

Confluence, like introjection, begins early in childhood. Some aspects of it are inevitable and not necessarily negative. Ordinary empathy enables us to identify mentally with the feelings and emotions of others, allowing us to understand them better. For example, a mother and infant represent a healthy form of confluence, where needs converge in an instinctual and loving relationship. However, the developmental task of growing children is to become increasingly able to take care of their own needs and become responsibly independent. This process is disrupted when insecure parents interfere through enmeshment. In this situation children do not learn clear boundaries and as adults typically seek partners who fit into a new confluent relationship that repeats the pattern of their childhood.

Gay partners of straight spouses are likely to have a pattern of confused boundaries as a strong defense against their own individuality. Many enter straight marriages believing they can give up their homosexuality. Bowing to social pressure, they may spend years hiding their sexual identity from others and even from themselves. They likely have internalized the societal message that it is wrong to be gay. They instinctively seek solace in a marriage where enmeshment is an unconscious place to hide. In the previous chapters, we saw examples of confluence in Jim and Stan and Joseph, all of whom married women they cared about, while denying their homosexuality and probably hoping to suppress it. Kit also covered her lesbian impulses through serial affairs with men, while clinging to her marriage with Phil.

Straight spouses often enter marriage with an entrenched pattern of confused boundaries. Because it takes "two to conflu'," people with this pattern tend to find each other. These partners ignore or gloss over differences. This leads to large blind spots in awareness where we block out information from our environment that does not match our ideals. "How could I have been so unaware of my mate's homosexuality?" was a common sentiment expressed in the interviews. When straight spouses confuse their partners' needs with their own, they eventually lose their sense of individual identity. This is devastating when they separate or divorce. Carol, for example, was completely disoriented when her roles as wife and business partner vanished at the same time. She had melded her identity with Jim's.

"We" language is often used in the confluent pattern in place of sentences that begin with "I." When the royal "we" is used to suggest a course of action, it is more difficult to disagree. Disagreement feels like betrayal in this unstated pattern of enmeshment. For example, saying, "We wouldn't want to hurt your mother's feelings by telling her I am gay" feels much more coercive than saying, "I don't want to hurt your mother by telling her I am gay." The "we" language, indicative of unhealthy and merged boundaries, absolves us of individual accountability for our feelings. Straight spouses may tell themselves, "We want to stay together," confusing this with personal desire for a loving, intimate relationship. Kaye and Joseph, in Chapter 2, are examples. In the long run, it is avoidance of responsibility for personal needs and desires. Couples who do stay in their mixed-orientation relationship often demonstrate this pattern.

Both straight spouses and their gay partners tend to be "helpers," trying to meet each other's needs without paying attention to their own. Both partners may take this role, or one may be the dominant "giver" and the other the primary "receiver." Whatever the relationship, it is helpful to become aware of underlying confluent patterns and work toward healing. A way to begin that healing is to identify smaller needs or interests, separate from your partner's. Choose for yourself which movie <u>you</u> want to see, what party <u>you</u> prefer to attend, or people <u>you</u> want to invite for dinner. Decide if you want a quiet night alone for reading or reflection. Or, if you follow your partner's preference, make it a conscious decision, based on both giving and receiving. These little choices seem quite daunting at first, but they provide a positive foundation for healing the effects of merged boundaries.

RETROFLECTION

Retroflection is a process that turns back on oneself that which the body would normally direct outward. A way to understand this defense mechanism is that you "Do unto yourself what you would really like to do to another person." This pattern may grow from fear of the consequences of expressing negative reaction to another's behavior. In the straight spouse dilemma, rather than showing anger toward your gay partner, retroflection turns the anger toward yourself. For example, you may chide yourself for "stupidity" for marrying someone who is homosexual, even though you didn't know.

The body's natural impulse directs anger out in order to be safe from threats of harm. This protective impulse is usually unnecessary because we are seldom in actual physical danger. But the brain and body register danger when faced with emotional threat as well. Our first response is often anger; then our bodies prepare physiologically for quick, defensive action. Some people are aware of this process as it happens, but because of upbringing or cultural training, many are not.

People who have learned to deny their feelings of anger often block the awareness of bodily sensations that would alert them to an activated state of physical defense. When anger arises and they are unconscious of it, the energy of the arousal can loop back on the body and do real harm. Many illnesses and accidents are a result of such retroflection. It can be seen in depression, stress-related diseases, nightmares, accidents, and anxiety. It is also present in self-derogatory statements, habits such as nail-biting, addictive behavior, eating disorders, and poor self-care. Kim's history, in Chapter 1, is a good illustration.

Childhood training often does not teach people to work with anger in a wholesome way that does not harm self or others. A straight spouse may be ill-equipped to handle tumultuous emotions that follow a partner's coming out, especially if their relationship reinforced denial of feelings. Often, straight spouses have spent years denying their needs, or not even recognizing them. They ignore bodily sensations that signal distress and accumulate unmet needs. This pattern may translate into rage that erupts outwardly or implodes in retroflection.

People who consistently deny feelings may suffer serious symptoms and significant health risk. Even those who are conscious of their anger sometimes turn the feelings back on themselves. Others experience waves of rage that seem overwhelming, or they may cycle through anger, grief, numbness, and denial. These intense emotional cycles can recur for years after the initial coming-out crisis.

Consciously working with emotions leads us to process anger and intense feelings in a way that hurts no one. This skill is not prevalent in our culture and is a challenge to most people. The confusing mixture of feelings in a complicated crisis more than doubles its difficulty. One simple method for addressing this challenge is to become aware of body signals that mark our preparation for physical defense. Then we must learn not to judge ourselves for this physiological arousal that is a natural survival mechanism. This retraining can be difficult because society labels the aroused state as "bad," associating it with destructive action. As conscious awareness grows, we can begin to avoid reactive behaviors and accept without judgment whatever thoughts arise. Combining self-awareness with kindness and understanding, we are less likely to turn defensive impulses against ourselves. We can begin to relax in the situation.

Several examples of the self-destructive tendency of retroflection can be found in previous chapters. Matt's self-deprecation and loss of energy, Kim's dependence on drugs, Kaye's arthritis, and Carol's high blood pressure may relate to negative energy denied and internalized.

PROJECTION

Projection is a process of attributing aspects of our internal world onto others. In this defense mechanism, individuals project their own traits or believed thoughts onto another person. Projection is very common in human interactions and may be the most unconscious of the boundary disturbances. For example, in order to protect ourselves from anger that we unconsciously deny, we imagine anger coming from the other person. Or perhaps a parent judged us harshly and we consequently suffer from a cruel inner critic, also seeing other people as judgmental—even if they are not. These are examples of projecting emotions or traits on someone else. Such projections cause great distress and confusion in relationships.

Straight spouses commonly experience their gay partner's sexual identification as a judgment or rejection of themselves. Some blame themselves and feel responsible for their mates' homosexuality. Their feelings may grow from fears and experiences rooted in childhood. All children and adults fear abandonment to some degree, and a troubled marriage deepens this fear. People who have actually experienced emotional or physical abandonment have even greater difficulty. Their feelings of judgment, rejection, and abandonment are exacerbated by their projections of the past onto the present.

Intimate partners often harm their relationship by projecting onto each other traits of other significant family members. Here's an example. A husband's subtle suggestion of sexual disinterest evokes his wife's childhood pain, caused by a depressed and emotionally unavailable parent. Nothing she could do as a child would interest her father in spending time with her. Years later, her husband's sexual indifference stirs up overwhelming feelings of abandonment and shame, incongruent with the mate's disinterest. In this example, the wife's internalized message of rejection from childhood is projected onto her husband, who "hooks" this particular feeling. The hook may be a similar personality trait or mannerism or action that evokes the parent or sibling who originally delivered the painful childhood message.

Childhood feelings of abandonment, triggered in the present by a partner's sexual disinterest, may turn into rage directed against self or others, or they may manifest as severe self-criticism or depression. As seen in our example, projection may amplify a subtle slight into complete rejection by the adult partner, just as the young girl interpreted her father's depression as indifference, dislike, or hatred of herself. Childhood imagination is still at work when we project early family experiences onto others who trigger similar negative feelings. These projections are exaggerated if derogatory comments, threats, or abuse were common in childhood.

Attempting to disown an internalized message through projection has one healthy component: Intuitively, we know that our negative self-attitude belongs outside, not inside, us. Unfortunately, projection also has a destructive side: Confusing a mate with someone from the past indicates blindness to reality. Like children who polarize their thoughts and feelings into good or bad, we imagine the worst about the intentions of others when we're threatened by conflict or separation.

This process of projection lies at the core of most troubled relationships. Like retroflection, which turns negative energy inward, projection involves energy that must be redirected appropriately, or it will surely cause harm. Projection is evident when intimate partners divide feelings unevenly, as when one partner expresses all the grief and the other partner expresses all the anger, or one mate carries all the feelings and the other none. In such instances, it is likely that each spouse has learned to project repressed feelings or unconscious attitudes onto the other, creating a very lopsided emotional load for each.

Many times, projection in the gay–straight spouse relationship is also deeply entangled with gender identities and social roles. Many partners unconsciously carry projected societal expectations and also project their own images of masculine and feminine behavior onto their partners. The upheaval of a partner's coming out may strongly challenge the straight spouse's role and cause a period of confusion over sexual identity. However the marriage is resolved, this crisis may become an opportunity for each individual to cultivate a new balance of skills and personal qualities that are associated with both the feminine and the masculine.

It is a great burden when we unconsciously carry a feeling that someone has projected onto us. As children, we have no choice. If parents repress all expression of a primary emotion, a child may assume this feeling for the whole family and then experience rejection for being the sad or angry one. When that child grows up, he or she may resume this old pattern of carrying the feelings that a marriage partner represses or disowns. When couples have to untangle their emotional lives, they are often shocked to discover their authentic feelings, apart from others' expectations and projections. Eventually, their shock may turn into relief, as they open to a fuller range of emotional awareness.

If you notice yourself carrying all the blame or projecting it all onto your partner, look deeply at your unconscious process of projection. If that pattern is present, treat yourself with kindness. Don't blame yourself for repeating behaviors passed down from generation to generation. You can learn to take responsibility for your own strengths and shortcomings. You can choose to psychologically return to others the feelings you no longer feel compelled to carry for them. In this way, you can ultimately contribute to your own happiness and the well-being of others.

DEFLECTION

The last defensive pattern, deflection, has as many healthy expressions as unhealthy ones. Without the ability to ward off a constant onslaught of external stimuli we would be unable to focus or concentrate our attention on any one thing. When we deflect, we turn away or divert our attention elsewhere. To deflect intimacy in relationship, we avoid eye contact, change the subject, space out, compulsively joke, work too much, spend too much, chronically forget commitments, or involve ourselves in myriad forms of obsessive behaviors. Extreme avoidance can turn inward and become self-destructive retroflection.

Children learn deflective behaviors to avoid painful interactions or in imitation of family members who avoided contact with them. As adults we continue this habituated pattern that leads to isolation in our current family relationships. A marriage may appear to be close, though partners actually feel a million miles apart and experience deep loneliness.

Living with someone who employs deflection as a major defense can be a source of confusion and frustration. Subtle avoidant behavior may leave us feeling not quite right, but not really knowing what is wrong. A person may offer a compliment but be looking the other way. The compliment may come with a voice inflection or joke that makes us question it later. It is common to counter a deflection with another deflection, pretending we didn't notice what seemed negative in the compliment. Pretending becomes unconscious over time, as we block awareness of the troubling behavior. These holes in awareness can exist for years in a marriage, until the shock of an illicit affair or other painful evidence of marital infidelity arises.

In a mixed-orientation marriage where the gay member has not come out, deflection is a common defense for both partners. The gay spouse unconsciously diverts contact to avoid confrontation or honesty, and the straight mate unconsciously deflects to avoid rejection or hurtful encounters. As painful as truth-telling can be, it is often a time when partners experience greater shared intimacy because the shields used to avoid each other come down. However, one or both partners may then feel too vulnerable, and the old patterns quickly return. In this case, protective shields turn into concrete walls.

Deflection is commonly used to blunt awareness of inner feelings and needs. We consume ourselves with constant motion or preoccupation with thoughts and activities. We wear down our ability to make conscious choices because we do not recognize genuine feelings and deeper desires. Lack of meaningful internal contact is reflected in shallow outer relationships. Constantly maintaining a polite persona in a marriage is a way of deflecting potential intimacy. Talking in generalities instead of specifics is another avoidance tool that keeps partners at a distance. Truth often hides in details that self-deflection averts. Learning to trust our senses requires slowing down, focusing on internal messages, and finding courage to face genuine feelings. The simple practice of slowing down and focusing on the breath may offer opportunity for meaningful contact with bodily experience, helping us relax and be more present for others as well.

CONCLUSION

Meaningful relationships are difficult at this time of crisis. Nothing is more important than genuine contact with others, while confronting confusion, shame, fear, despair, rage, or feeling totally shut down. You come to understand that you cannot change your spouse; you can only change yourself. At first, this may seem terribly unfair and hard to imagine. Yet through kindness, self-awareness, and positive action, you discover strength to manage difficult emotions. Recognizing and outgrowing outdated defense mechanisms through the suggested exercises can modify psychological patterns that have become obstacles.

This chapter's discussion of boundary disturbances and coping patterns serves as background for Chapter 5's examination of fear and shame, two emotional challenges that come up immediately after a spouse comes out. Stories from the interviews alternate with analysis from the therapist's perspective.

QUESTIONS TO PONDER

Introjection

1. What societal introject have I assumed without questioning? Does it fit for me? Do I choose to keep it, alter it, or reject it?
2. What family messages were positive? What family messages were negative? Is there an old tape that makes it difficult to like myself or make good choices for myself?
3. What positive message would I choose for myself at this time of difficulty?

Confluence

1. Is it difficult to know what I truly want?
2. Do I have a hard time making decisions when others are involved?
3. Do I let others choose for me?
4. Do I notice myself, family members, or my spouse using the word "we" to express an individual opinion, choice, or desire?

Retroflection

1. Do I have physical mannerisms or symptoms that may be rooted in retroflection?
2. Am I prone to accidents, illness, or injuries at this time? Are chronic physical problems worse than usual?
3. Do I seldom or never feel the emotion of anger in my body?
4. Do I say negative things to myself when something goes wrong in my environment or with other people?
5. Do I judge myself harshly for being in a relationship with someone who is gay?

Projection

1. Am I in a relationship where the expression of feelings is distributed in a lopsided manner? Is this a family pattern for me or for my spouse?
2. Is there one particular emotion, such as anger or grief, that I do not express? Is there an emotion that I continually feel and/or

express? Am I unable to feel anything? Are any of these patterns of behavior in evidence in other family members, now or in my childhood? What about my partner's family?

3. How is the difficult behavior of my spouse like one of my parents or siblings? What unfinished business with this family member intensifies my painful emotional response to my mate?

Deflection

1. Do I use deflection to avoid staying with emotions, bodily sensations, or intuitions? How do I do this?
2. Do I use deflection to avoid contact with others? How do I do this?
3. What deflective behaviors do I observe in my partner and others in my immediate circle at this time? How do their actions affect how I feel and respond?

ACTIVITIES

Introjection

1. Write down several believed thoughts that are presently getting in your way. Try to identify their original source. For a period of one to four weeks make a commitment to notice how one of these repeated ideas enters your thinking or behaviors throughout the day. Be gentle with yourself! When you become aware of an introject, appreciate your new awareness and replace it with a positive message to yourself. Note in your journal when you were able to practice this awareness exercise and how you felt. This is a challenging practice; congratulate yourself even for small progress.
2. Continue this practice with other internalized messages you have identified. This exercise can be particularly helpful after a difficult encounter with your spouse, friend, or family member that may trigger shame or self-blame.

Confluence

1. If this is a boundary disturbance you struggle with, commit to bring conscious awareness to confluent speech and behaviors in yourself and others. Replace the word "we" with "I" and notice how it feels. Be patient with yourself and others in the process. Every time you detect the pattern, appreciate your new awareness and write in your journal about your feelings and experiences.
2. Notice how you feel when others use the royal "we." Remember that the word received royal connotation because kings and queens assumed the court was always aligned with their sentiments and needs! Nevertheless, in this exercise it is not your job to correct others. Instead, be wary of messages that blur your boundaries and confuse your relationships. You can learn to see the habit clearly and decide instead to define yourself independently, even in the face of resistance. Communication tools appear later in the book to offer more effective language.
3. Each day select an activity that is specifically tailored to your own needs and desires. Start small. Record the activities and your progress in your journal.

Retroflection

1. If you answer yes to any of these questions, make a commitment to address one of your retroflective behaviors in the next one to four weeks. Begin by cultivating daily awareness of its presence in your thoughts or body. Remember that this new awareness is not another opportunity to beat yourself up! Instead, appreciate your progress. If the retroflection is a tension, pain, or habit in your body, focus your attention into the area, slow your breathing, and relax for a moment. If the pattern occurs in your thoughts, notice what you say to yourself and let it go. Then replace your self-inflicted negativity with kind and positive words.
2. Write in your journal about your experiences with these exercises, noting any small changes in thoughts and actions. Deep-seated patterns will take time to reverse, but recognize that any new awareness indicates beneficial progress.

Projection

1. When issues from the family of origin compound a current relationship crisis, the challenge can be daunting and overwhelming. First, understand that most marriage and family difficulties are entangled with our cultural, personal, and childhood histories. This basic understanding helps us see beyond self-blame and recrimination. Next, commit to identifying one pattern of behavior that has its roots in the process of projection. Notice what emotion is most tied to this behavior. Also note internal self-talk about your actions and feelings. Write observations in your journal and share your insights with a close friend or counselor.

2. Practice identifying a pattern of projection in your daily actions for one to four weeks. Each time, remind yourself that your response is influenced or intensified by past experience. Slowly breathe to help relax in the moment. After practicing this exercise for a while you will begin to notice that your emotional response lessens over time.

   NOTE: This exercise is not suggested if you have serious abuse or neglect in your family history, as it may compound or intensify your emotional response. If you discover this occurring, you should seek professional help.

Deflection

1. Choose one deflective behavior (avoidance pattern) you have identified in yourself that you would like to change. Commit to gently bring attention to moments when you automatically engage in this habit. At first you may feel dismayed or judge yourself for how often you notice your pattern. Conscious attention to this defense mechanism will eventually decrease its frequency.

   After a couple of weeks you may add a means of contact that your behavior was cutting short. For example, if you avoid eye contact, make an effort to look more directly when talking with someone else. If you notice a tendency to change the subject when the conversation feels personal, allow yourself to stay a little longer with your feelings and the topic at hand.

It's a good idea to begin this exercise when your emotions are not highly charged and with individuals who do not feel threatening. Remember that small changes can make a big difference. Increased contact can bring you closer to people who could help you at this time. Your journal can also be a good friend when you write down your feelings and observations on a regular basis.

2. When you notice how others habitually deflect their attention, concentrate awareness on your own feelings and reactions to their behavior. Dispassionate observance opens more options for response. For example, if your partner often changes the subject, you can bring the conversation back to the central topic. It is better to assert your own interests, rather than trying to change someone else by labeling him or her "wrong."

This exercise is useful with friends and family who want to be supportive yet have deflective patterns that obstruct healing. Such people may avoid contact, change the subject, or suggest that you not cry. Identify at least one person as a close contact when you need to share feelings. Say that you need to cry or talk and just have someone listen for a short time. If there is no one in your circle who is capable of learning this skill, it is important to find a counselor or therapist, so you don't feel completely alone.

Chapter 5

Immediate Personal Challenges

FEAR, SECRECY, AND ISOLATION

How can I go on alone, after all this time being with her? Hal asked himself when his wife of twenty years came out. He voiced the primary fear most straight mates feel: *I'll grow old alone and lonely.* Carol remembers it this way: *The week Jim moved out of our home, I remember catching my breath in the grocery store, eyes full of tears, when I saw an elderly couple walking hand in hand. That will never be me, I thought.* This sense of abandonment was voiced in various ways by most of the straight spouses in this book, and it translates into a complexity of fears.

In the confused time after homosexual mates come out, fear is the greatest enemy. There are layers of loss. Decisions driven by fear often have negative results. Everything that matters most is in danger—family relationships, welfare of children, personal health, home, financial security, friends, social standing, reputation, sometimes career and livelihood. Worst of all is the possibility of losing one's very identity. Carol experienced all of these anxieties. *When my marriage ended, my business career also evaporated. In order to divide our assets, we had to sell our family business, a jointly owned staffing company. For a long time afterward, I lost my sense of self. I was a refugee in my mind. The future was murky and I was afraid that all my roots had been severed.* Such fear is at the core of other paralyzing realities, notably, secrecy and the isolation that it creates. Claire's story is another good example.

Claire had been married to Don for thirty-eight years when she learned of his homosexuality. Their union was never sexually satisfying to Claire and she always sensed some barrier that she couldn't un-

When Your Spouse Comes Out
Published by The Haworth Press, Taylor & Francis Group, 2008. All rights reserved.
doi:10.1300/6046_05

derstand. She says, *We were more like siblings than spouses, and like the boss and the secretary. He was not able to tell me he loved me; he did not like physical affection, kissing on the lips, for example, and he gagged and bolted the first time I French-kissed him. Obviously, he was able to have sex with me, as we do have four children, but there was never any romance in our sexual relationship, and I missed that and resented the lack of it. I felt like a receptacle and often cried myself to sleep after our sexual encounters.* Like most other straight spouses, Claire recalls blaming herself: *I wished I knew what was wrong with me.*

Claire's discovery of her husband's homosexuality came when she returned from an out-of-town conference and had a very odd conversation with a friend. *He told me there was something I should know about my husband. This person was so distraught about telling me that he wanted to write to an advice columnist first, and then said that he was going out of town for a few days! After a very sleepless night, I encountered the person again the next day and said that I could not be left hanging. He still felt unable to tell me. After a little back-and-forthing, I said, "Does this have anything to do with sexual orientation?" Until I heard the words come out of my mouth, I did not know what I was going to say. After a very long time, and with a huge sense of relief, the person said, "Yes." I still do not know where my question came from but believe that during the night my unconscious processed dozens of clues from more than thirty-eight years and came up with what I should have known all along.*

It was an "aha" experience for Claire. *That explains everything! I had an overwhelming feeling of relief, of having the answer to so much—maybe all that was so awry in our relationship.* Armed with her new insight, Claire forged ahead. *It took me two days to process the information and confront Don. I did so on Monday afternoon. He wanted to talk about our upcoming trip to Italy. I suggested that we sit down to talk and said that I didn't want to travel with him. Then I asked him point-blank if he were gay. Don neither confirmed nor denied it. Instead, he ducked the question and said, "I have always loved you in my own way."*

Don's unwillingness to acknowledge his sexual orientation emerged in this very first confrontation, and it persists to this day. Claire remembers that three days after she asked her direct question, *Don announced he was moving to Phoenix and would be leaving the next morning to go there to find an apartment.* Two months passed before he returned, packed his things, and moved out of the family's home.

When Claire and Don separated, the couple's four sons ranged in age from twenty-six to thirty-six and were no longer living at home. However, a younger child was in the picture. Claire and Don had taken responsibility for one son's daughter when she was just a year old and her parents were divorcing under very problematic circumstances. The grandparents had provided the little girl a stable home for eight years. Having a nine-year-old at home complicated Claire's situation. She was automatically drawn into Don's closet of secrecy.

Don's greatest fear was being found out. He wanted no one to know, and I said that I would not out him to his family members. With this promise to keep Don's secret, Claire isolated herself from the family and most of her friends. Truth was a luxury that she agreed to give up. This was especially painful in her conversations with Don's family. *He was primarily concerned about his sister and brother and extended family finding out. One of our sons learned, however, and the news traveled from one to another. Now all four children know. I still have not said anything to Don's relatives, even though they are very curious about what happened to dissolve a thirty-eight-year marriage. I have been dragged into the closet, and I don't like it, and I don't like the fact that they may be thinking it is my fault.*

It is hard enough for an adult to understand and accept the discovery of hidden homosexuality, but it's even harder to explain to a child. Claire also faced that hurdle. *It took me many months to process things enough to be able to tell my granddaughter, but she has been completely accepting of it all in the way that children can be. She only wishes that her grandpa could talk about it.*

There's the rub. Don won't face this issue. *He is still in the darkest corner of his closet,* Claire says. *He lies constantly.* The two of them are still legally married, though they have been separated for four years. Don seems utterly uprooted. *He lives all over the place,* Claire says. He spent last summer in New York, returned to Arizona, stayed with their son in Colorado until the two of them had a falling out, and now is living in a rental in a small town not far from Claire's city. *He can't get along with his kids and is losing touch with the whole family. He's never seen our two-year-old grandson in Oregon, though he travels all over the place. Why can't he fly to Oregon to see his own grandchild? He has had a tortured life by living in the closet and not being able to be true to himself. It has done irreparable harm to so many of his relationships.*

During the early months after the separation, Claire was most worried that she would have to move. She wrote, *I feared the probability of having to sell my house, which I love, and which is the only home and security my granddaughter has known. The neighbors have been an extended family for us. The whole process of relocating seems overwhelming at this point in my life, and I don't like feeling forced into it.*

Claire managed to keep her home during the following four years, providing coveted stability for her granddaughter, but it was very difficult. *I am living a whole lot poorer, as we are suddenly supporting Don's separate apartment and his extensive and constant travel. My own work as a freelance artist is not enough to support life, especially as most of my time and energy go to caring for Amy and being primary caretaker for my mother, who is ninety-five and in the late stages of Alzheimer's. I'm ready for it to be over with but just can't get around to filing for divorce.*

Claire's history shows three personal challenges that straight spouses typically face early on: fear, secrecy, and the resulting isolation. Her greatest fear when Don left was losing her home, which represented her own roots as well as Amy's shelter from the turmoil of her parents' situation. Money worries were immediate. The house was expensive to maintain, and her occupation as an artist couldn't support the two of them. Her income was greatly reduced with Don's departure, and she was unable to take more lucrative jobs because of additional family calamities that came all at once: her mother's Alzheimer's, her daughter's ovarian cancer, her son's heart attack, and the death of her younger brother—which came just two weeks after Don moved out. Claire shudders now at the memory of her multiple traumas.

Daily living in the closet of secrecy was just as debilitating. The necessity to edit her communications with everyone in the family to protect Don's secret was a huge burden. *My lowest point was realizing that my husband was an adroit liar, and I had to question everything he had said to me over all the years of our marriage. I had always trusted him to tell me the truth, and loss of that trust was devastating.* Secrecy and duplicity took its toll. Claire said at the time, *Emotionally, I am strung out. Mentally, I have so many "senior moments" that I am starting to feel daffy.*

Isolation is often a result of sharing the closet with a gay mate. Both are in hiding. Claire's "daffy" feeling is not unusual. Many straight spouses fear for their sanity during this phase. They feel separated from their friends—different. Often they feel dirty and ashamed. When they are able to speak truthfully, even with one person—a friend or relative or therapist—it helps immensely. Claire confirms it in her experience: *What keeps me from dissolving onto the floor is that I have a network of the most extraordinary friends, a book group, hiking group, dream group, calligraphers' guild, volunteer activities with my dog, and a couple of good solitaire games on the computer.* Apparently, Claire is coping with her pain by reaching out to trusted friends and occupying her time with constructive activities. She's on a track to recovery. Claire's history demonstrates a number of experiences common to straight spouses. In the next section, we'll see how a clinical psychologist might guide clients through this phase of the process.

A THERAPEUTIC APPROACH TO FEAR

Fear is the emotion at the root of all physiological reactions of fight, flight, or freeze (LeDoux, 1996), responding to real or perceived threat. Sorting out real from imaginary danger is key to lessening the strength of heightened reactions that induce isolation, somatic stress, strain in relationships, and hopelessness over time. Learning to listen to signals of fear in our bodies can help us make better choices that are not reactive in the moment. Learning to respect and work with fear without allowing it to take over is a crucial step in the process. A conscious choice to protect ourselves from others when a spouse first acknowledges homosexuality does not mean we have to isolate from everyone or forever. Rather, we can make new decisions based on incoming internal and external information.

Reinforcing fears through imagination, thoughts, and behaviors may sink us into depression, as well as advance the hopeless outcomes we imagine. If we continually envision the same disastrous future, repeatedly rerunning fears, it is imperative to stop the cycle by looking objectively at our emotions.

For example, AIDS is a real danger for straight mates. If fear about it takes over, you may become so frozen you cannot act, or you could flee from the issue in denial or expend all your energy fighting your partner instead of facing the real possibility of disease. Fear of social rejection might send you into friendless isolation, avoiding social interactions. Instead, use the positive aspects of the fight, flight, or freeze response to mobilize self-care. Say "no" to unsafe sex and get a health check. Use energy proactively to seek others who can help. These are ways to take positive, protective action.

Awareness

Fear is like a train that we must stop, look, and listen for to avoid being run over. This is the awareness phase of the work, a first major step toward healing. Ending compulsive busyness and runaway thoughts, then slowing down to breathe more deeply can help us hear the whistle signal of fear. In a sense, reactive behaviors isolate us from ourselves. By learning to recognize the early signs of dread in our bodies we can avert the build-up of anxiety that leads to a downward spiral of negative thoughts, isolation, overwhelming exhaustion, or panicked actions. Learning to respect and appreciate fear is part of the awareness phase. The less we judge our physiological responses, the more we are actually able to simply observe the emotion and calm ourselves when frightened. Awareness involves experiencing both our bodies and thoughts in a mindful way.

Insight

Awareness leads to insight, the second phase of this healing process. As our awareness of internal states increases, we may more accurately perceive the external environment. This is because we are better able to separate the two. As our observations become clearer, our mental outlook also synthesizes and expands possibilities. We discover that our mental pictures of future loneliness and ruin are only thoughts, not reality. Though we may feel quite lonely at the moment, forced into the closet where many dreams have been dashed, insight based on awareness can help us realize that the present situation is not necessarily a forecast of the future. Most of our frightening thoughts are just fueling unreasonable fear and reactive expressions of fight, flight, or freeze.

Action

The third phase of healing is marked by action. Insight naturally leads to the act of decision making, provided we stay in the flow and diligently keep our attention on both internal and external realities. We can monitor our experience of fear and at the same time decide to take our first steps to move through suffering and into genuine relationship. While allowing a natural process to run its course, we can also choose to ride the waves of our emotions in a boat we are making sturdy. Remembering to slow down and breathe may be our first action step. It is so simple and works so well it is worth repeating and remembering for the rest of our lives.

One easy method of monitoring our thoughts without judgment can be the practice of labeling them as past or future, then gently coming back to the present moment with attention to the breath. Another method is to examine thoughts about the past and to notice if our ruminations are fueling anger or hopelessness or truly helping us review, grieve, and let go. A method for working with future thoughts is to notice if we are problem solving and envisioning possibilities, or if we have spiraled into worry and negative images. Whether we are thinking of the past or future, a final method is to notice when the mental tape or picture is negative, stop the process without self-judgment, then replace the negative picture or words with a calming image or soothing phrase.

Positive actions can move from an internal focus to external deeds of self-care and developing trusting relationships. For a person frozen with fear, getting off the couch to take a walk or call a friend may be a first act of courage in reversing isolation and despair. When caught in a manic state of flight, resting on the couch while slowing the breath may be important. Slowing down encourages awareness of grief that frantic activity masks. If you are prone to the fight response, write antagonistic feelings and observations in your journal to monitor impulses of aggression. Identify when you tend to fight, flee, or freeze in response to fear and its subtle variations of discomfort, anxiety, distress, or panic. Some individuals lean heavily into one mode of fear response, and others may shift between two or three. Getting acquainted with your own patterns can help begin the three-step healing process of awareness, insight, and action.

The final stage of action has a feedback loop through awareness and insight. This allows an opportunity to stop to observe the results of our actions. We can then decide to make corrections or continue on with the positive results we are reaping. It has been said that a rocket ship is off course more than 90 percent of the time. It continually veers a little off the exact path and then corrects itself toward its target. This metaphor may help us accept the missteps on our personal journey to recovery. Anyone trying new behaviors is in an experimental process that can be frightening, but like the rocket, our course can be corrected as we go. Watching our attitudes toward the unknown can help us work with the balance of excitement and anxiety that new opportunities provoke. Taking small steps at first can provide a sense of safety and community to give us courage to reach incrementally larger goals.

Let's review the three-step healing process to work with these early emotional challenges. Nonjudgmental <u>awareness</u> is the fundamental antidote for fears that spawn secrecy and isolation. Reach for the root of feelings by sensing the body and monitoring thoughts. Observe others with curiosity and a little distance to read their behaviors without arousing the confusing filter of fear. When awareness shines a clear light on the disabling quality of isolating and secretive behaviors, we enter the second phase of healing: <u>insight</u>. Insight, or true understanding, expands options and enables us to solve problems. We are better able to connect the dots because we see more possibilities and are not fixated by fear. With awareness and insight, we are armed for <u>action</u> in the world. Encourage authentic engagement with self and others by making initial decisions. Find someone to trust, take small but significant steps, and frequently review previous actions.

The same three-step healing process of <u>awareness, insight, and action</u> applies to other immediate emotional challenges illustrated in the rest of this chapter. Before we examine those topics, here is a checklist of action steps that may alleviate fear.

1. <u>Awareness of Fear</u>
   - Watch for fight behaviors:
     —Feelings of irritation, frustration, anger, and rage
     —Arguments; snippy, sarcastic, or backbiting comments
     —Hurting yourself (retroflections)

- Watch for flight behaviors:
  —Compulsive busyness or overwork
  —Denial (saying things like, "It's not that bad," or "My partner will change")
  —Distractions (watching too much TV, caretaking others instead of yourself)
- Watch for freeze behaviors:
  —Holding your breath
  —Numbed feelings
  —Isolating and keeping secrets
  —Inability to get out of bed, off the couch, or out of the house

2. Insight into Fear
   - Watch how your thoughts connect to bodily sensations.
   - Learn from self-observation your primary reactive defense patterns.
   - Use knowledge of your fear patterns for self-understanding, not self-rebuke.
   - Realize that your present situation is not the future.
   - Talk with others experienced in the loss and personal crisis of gay–straight relationships.

3. Action Steps to Counter Fear
   - Actively and systematically witness sensations, thoughts, and behaviors. Commit to check in with your internal process three times throughout the day and write your observations in a daily journal.
   - Remember to slow down and breathe when you're aware of a fear response.
   - Without judgment, label thoughts "past" or "future," then come back to the present moment by bringing your attention to slowing your breath.
   - Without judgment, notice if thoughts of the past are fueling anger or hopelessness, or if they are helping you move forward. It can be useful to set aside a special time of day to review and grieve. This can assist you in containing the largest feelings to keep them from erupting when you are on the job, with your children, or during other activities.

- Again, without judgment, notice if thoughts about the future hold negative images, or if you are problem solving and envisioning better possibilities.
- Immediately replace negative mental images with a calming image. Create a simple mental picture that represents peace to you. It can be anything that's personally comforting, perhaps a favorite mountain lake, a calm ocean, or a gentle butterfly. Consistently use this mental picture to replace one that is disturbing or painful.
- When you notice negative self-talk, immediately repeat a phrase that reminds you of a centered, peaceful state. It could be wisdom borrowed from a poem or religious tradition or a simple sentence like, "Peace is in my heart." Use the same phrase repeatedly to replace self-criticism and inward scorn.

Recognize the clear progression of awareness, insight, and action, and use the proactive suggestions given here to encourage positive progress through all the straight spouse stages of recovery.

SHAME AND SELF-DOUBT

Something was always missing in our marriage, and I always thought it was my fault. I must not be good enough, somehow. This is a common sentiment expressed by many straight spouses in the interviews. Emily put it this way: *There was always an emotional distance between us, and that made me feel dissatisfied and led to sexual dissatisfaction. Sex seemed to be merely a physical release for him, and I thought I was lacking something.* When Emily's husband disclosed his homosexuality, she felt a certain odd relief. Like other straight spouses, she had always felt some nameless inadequacy. Her first reaction was, *Whew! Then it wasn't me!* It wasn't that she wasn't pretty enough, or sexy enough, or smart enough. It wasn't about her at all.

But long-cultivated seeds of self-doubt continue to grow in the minds of many straight spouses, producing the bitter fruit of shame. Low self-esteem is a common problem. After the initial relief of disclosure passes, there is usually a period of "feeling stupid." One woman spoke for many: *What kind of a freak am I to choose a gay husband! How could I miss something so basic? I should have known sooner.*

Such self-recrimination feeds the fear of what other people will think and this fear drives the wounded partner further into lonely isolation. Carol remembers, *For a long time after Jim and I divorced, I avoided social contacts and retreated to the quiet refuge of home. Eventually I began dating an old friend. Though I felt safe with him, my fragile confidence was further shaken when he told me, "My friends think I'm brave to go out with you." The fact that people "out there" saw me as a health threat was a shock to me. I felt tainted. I saw myself as a social pariah, even though I carefully monitored my health and had clean results in the lab tests for the HIV virus and other sexually transmitted diseases.*

As months passed, I began to overcome my negative self-image, working with a therapist and reaching out to close friends for encouragement. Bad news does dissipate. Though I live in a relatively small city, my divorce and "horrible scandal" soon were replaced by the next tidbit of gossip. How long does a headline in a newspaper last? Even huge world crises eventually go away. In a personal crisis, our repeated mental story line *(What kind of a freak am I?)* is much more destructive than the outer events. The negative stories we tell ourselves are just thoughts, and it's a fact that we can change our thoughts.

One particularly perceptive straight spouse, Sandy, demonstrates the fruit of counseling, introspection, and gleaning the wisdom of voracious reading on the subject. Her thoughts on shame are instructive. *Ironically, the end of my marriage was the first major public failure of my life. Although it was humiliating and perhaps even carried a measure of shame, in the long run I learned that I can fail and survive and that many people loved me in spite of, and perhaps because of, my fallibility.* Perfection is neither required nor possible, though Sandy admits, *Getting to "good enough" has not been easy.*

In order to heal self-doubt, straight spouses must come to one deep understanding: We are neither stupid nor personally diminished because we partnered with a homosexual. The truth about their sexuality was simply hidden from us. We are not at fault because we were deceived, even about something so basic. Therefore, self-reproach is pointless and destructive. The famous Serenity Prayer can be a mantra to heal personal shame: "God grant me the serenity to accept the things I cannot change, the courage to change the things I can, and the wisdom to know the difference." Carol taped a copy of the prayer to her computer monitor. Now, years later, it remains there in full view, a reminder not to agonize over that which she cannot control.

A THERAPEUTIC APPROACH TO SHAME

The pattern of shame has its roots in early childhood development. Between ages two and three, children recognize good and bad, but not all the shades in between. They are also incapable of separating the doer from the deed. Thus, even the most loving parents may utter shaming exclamations, such as "You know better than that!" (The child hears, "That was stupid!" or "How dumb!") Repeated strong reprimands or repeated nonverbal messages of rejection instill shameful feelings in children. As we grow older, subtle or strong aggression or rejection can elicit a shame-based response the way it did in the past. If we are exposed as children to such debilitating messages, we are even more vulnerable to shame as adults. Culture reinforces shame for behaviors labeled as socially unacceptable. Shame may be invoked with avoidance of contact as in deflection, a disapproving glance, a snide remark, or overt criticism or attack.

Whether the expression is conscious or unconscious, shaming actions seek to control others and are often expressed in dominating behaviors. The shamed one internalizes the childhood message of rejection (introjection) and turns it into self-punishment (retroflection), self-neglect, or relentless inner critical thoughts. Nonverbal gestures, such as hanging the head, averting the face to avoid eye contact, and submissive behaviors, may indicate feelings of shame. Perfectionism and rigid self-control are also common signs of shame lurking beneath the surface. Even when childhood experiences of shame are minimal, continued exposure to subtle shame-inducing gestures or statements can erode self-confidence in adults. Because marriage has such strong influence on self-image, daily negative input can devastate a straight mate's sense of worth.

The gay partner also carries a tremendous burden of shame from society. Negative social values are expressed through homophobic jokes, innuendos, and pressure from family, the workplace, media, and friends. Insidious, unspoken messages of shame are often the most difficult to identify and address. This burden of rejection and hostility from the outside may be unconsciously brought home through the gay partner's diminished sense of self and reactive behaviors day-to-day. It would be impossible not to transfer some negative feelings to the straight spouse over time. Recognizing and labeling shame as a major contributing factor to the behavior of both partners affords greater perspective and the possibility of heartfelt compassion.

Secrecy is a strong component of shame, manifested in hiding and avoidance. Moreover, living in the closet reinforces humiliation. Hiding sexual identity is an expression of fear, based on a combination of flight and freeze behaviors. But any alternative can be dangerous. As recent violent events remind us, in parts of the United States and around the world, homosexuality can be a life-threatening identification. In some unenlightened places, gays are physically attacked, even tortured and killed. Mortal danger necessitates secrecy. At the very least, both partners may be at risk of losing their jobs, home, financial security, community, family, and friends. Children in the family may also suffer ridicule, rejection, and feelings of shame. The decision for either partner to come out of the closet therefore threatens everyone in the family.

If the gay or straight partner decides to tell the truth publicly, some general advice may ease the journey. It should be done with great care, timing, and sensitivity for the partner, the immediate family, and everyone involved. Before coming out to anyone beyond a close friend or therapist, address any inner sense of shame through counseling. Make realistic, cautious decisions, grounded on the observed attitudes of family, workplace, and community. However, making decisions based exclusively on the outer world relinquishes one's freedom to exist. It's equally essential to rely on personal inner wisdom to reach final conclusions about taking such an important step.

Bringing shame to awareness and naming it can do a great deal to alleviate the heavy weight of its oppression. Recognizing shaming introjects in negative self-talk and behaviors is as important as identifying past and current sources of shaming in your life. The spectrum of shame ranges from self-doubt to low self-esteem to self-loathing. Where you fall on that spectrum on any given day is an important indicator to note in your journal. A nonjudgmental attitude toward yourself in this investigation is crucial. Attention, patience, and kindness toward your own thoughts and hiding behaviors should bring immediate internal relief. However, if relentless, intense self-loathing persists, it should be addressed in psychotherapy.

Learning to shun rigid "good" and "bad" categories brings greater insight to your process of healing. Begin by simply noticing how you categorize thoughts and actions. It's useful to replace labeling everything as "good" or "bad" with objective observation and curiosity toward the source of those judgments. Notice the difference between outside opinion and what you truly value. This awareness can help you drop whole categories of judgment as you discern which thoughts and actions reinforce your values and which do not. A mindful process, based more on logic than prejudgment, offers greater self-understanding and opens choices you may otherwise have rejected.

Self-doubt can make the action of decision making difficult or impossible. Making decisions based on shame is seldom in our best interest and usually leads to deep inner turmoil. Talking through feelings of shame with a confidant(e) can help identify judgments of good and bad. Take sufficient time to reevaluate the situation and recognize the possibility of changing your mind. This openness can ease pressure to make an impossible, "perfect" choice.

Acts of self-love become important reminders of our essential value and worth. These can range from maintaining self-care habits to enjoying activities that might normally feel indulgent. Activities like going for a walk or taking a soaking bath can reduce stress and reinforce relaxation that might otherwise be out of grasp during a crisis. Spend more time with friends—or more time alone—depending on personal inclination. Make regular appointments for massage to ease exaggerated tension.

It is even more important to replace shaming self-talk with statements of care and love. Monitoring this internal dialogue, appreciate your courage in confronting your shame. This is an important step. Another essential step is to choose a brief phrase that addresses your particular issues of humiliation or self-doubt. Some examples are, "I value myself," "I am worthy of respect," and "I belong." Whenever shame threatens your balance, repeat your affirming phrase with encouraging energy. Affirming phrases can also be used when encountering other people's behaviors that trigger self-doubt or insecurity.

Guidelines from Marshall Rosenberg's (2005) teachings in *Nonviolent Communication* can be most helpful in giving voice to our feelings and need for respect and appropriate consideration from others.

This system provides a helpful structure for making requests without putting others on the defense or subjugating our needs to theirs. A simple four-step process follows:

1. Describe the behavior that is troublesome in your interactions. Learn to state the facts in an objective manner that does not blame, globalize, nor exaggerate. Instead of saying, "You always shut me down," state exactly what happened. For example, "When you tell me not to cry . . . ," or "When you frown and turn your body away . . ."
2. State how you feel. Use words that describe feelings instead of an image of what the other person is doing. Instead of saying, "I feel you are rejecting me," or "I feel that you aren't listening," say, "I feel sad," or "I feel disappointed," or "I feel angry." This helps the other person get inside your experience and understand you better.
3. State your fundamental need directly and positively. Needs are not something dependent on another person's particular action. Instead of saying, "I need your undivided attention," simply make a statement such as, "I need respect," or "I need gentleness." Others can relate to universal needs much better than a statement that sounds like a demand on them.
4. Make a request that is doable, present centered, and specific. This way you are much more likely to get your underlying needs met. Instead of demanding something nebulous like, "Quit being so hurtful," ask, "Would you be willing to face me and sit quietly for ten minutes as I describe my experience of anger and pain?" or "Would you be willing to not suggest I stop crying and instead ask me what would be most helpful in the moment?"

Because this action step of communicating effectively follows awareness and insight it may take some time before you have the information you need to spell out your observations, feelings, needs, and requests so clearly. It can also take some practice to do this with grace. Please don't judge yourself in the meantime. Remember, it is vital to begin asking for the respect and care you deserve.

The histories of Claire and Emily and others cited in this chapter illustrate key therapeutic principles behind this clinical approach. More personal stories in the next chapter will be similarly interpreted.

1. Awareness of Shame
   - Identify shame-based introjects in negative self-talk and behaviors.
   - Identify past and current sources of shaming. Notice the specific actions of others that trigger shame feelings. Does this remind you of someone in your past?
   - Track your self-esteem several times each day for a week. Confident? Doubting? Insecure? Low opinion of self? Self-loathing? Objectivity grows as you note fluctuations in your sense of self, and close observation demonstrates that feelings are not permanent.
   - Identify words or actions of your friends, family, or spouse that arouse shame.
   - Learn to recognize shame based on homophobic societal messages you receive in association with your mate.
   - Regularly note in your journal your awareness of these categories of shame. Getting it out of your system and onto paper is healing in itself.
2. Insight into Shame
   - Observe whether you rigidly categorize thoughts and actions into good or bad. Gently replace this labeling with observation and curiosity toward the source of these judgments.
   - Note the difference between your old mental tapes (introjects) and your own present values. Make a list of your values and which thoughts and actions support these principles. Note what undermines them.
   - Replace labeling thoughts and actions as "good" and "bad" with "helpful" and "unhelpful."
   - Distinguish between rules or standards you have been given and which ones make sense at this time in your life. Notice when you are a perfectionist or a rebel against the rules. Decide what is "good enough" by your own standards.
3. Action Steps to Counter Shame
   - Talk through feelings of shame with a psychotherapist.
   - Allow yourself time to make important decisions. Do not make decisions based on shame. Recognize the possibility of changing your mind.

- Maintain self-care habits throughout crisis periods and when you feel low. Resist the tendency to drop healthful activities when under stress.
- Practice the four-step process to communicate your fundamental needs and make requests. Read *Nonviolent Communication* by Marshall Rosenberg (2005) to increase your effectiveness and confidence.
- Increase activities that reduce stress and promote relaxation. Take more walks, hot baths, and time alone or with friends and pets. Listen to music, read, bake, garden, or do whatever you enjoy that does not impose outside pressure.
- Make regular appointments for massage and other health tune-ups.
- Appreciate yourself for recognizing shame-based introjects. Create a brief positive statement to replace a core negative message you have identified (such as "I value myself," "I am worthy of respect," "I belong"). Repeat it immediately whenever you experience shame.

Chapter 6

Lingering Risks, Anger, and Grief

PHYSICAL HEALTH RISKS

Unprotected sex in the marriage bed puts an unsuspecting straight spouse in real danger when the mate engages in clandestine homosexual activity. Carol, for example, was unaware of the threat: *When Jim came out to me in 1991, he had been having secret, anonymous sex with multiple partners for more than twenty years. He hid his homosexual activity so completely that I had no reason to suspect his fidelity during those years. I assumed that we had a stable, monogamous marriage. Not so. Without knowing, I had an extreme health risk during most of our years together.*

Emily, a fifty-three-year-old Canadian elementary teacher, wrote, *My worst time was the day I discovered my husband had given me crabs. This was after we had stopped being intimate but were still sharing the same bed. I have no words to describe how humiliated I felt. That day, I remember feeling like I couldn't put one foot in front of the other to go out and get what I needed to take care of myself.*

Emily somehow mustered the strength to do the right thing. *I visited my beautiful, caring family doctor. She was so kind to me. In all my life, I never thought I would need the tests she ordered that day—tests for AIDS and a cocktail of other sexually transmitted diseases. It was the blackest day of my life.* Fortunately, Emily was not HIV positive, but she could have been. Despite newer treatments for the disease, AIDS is still a major—and growing—threat.

Since 1981, when AIDS was first identified as a new disease, it has become the fourth leading cause of death worldwide. The United Nations estimates that 4.1 million people were newly infected with the virus that causes AIDS during 2005 and 2.8 million people lost their

When Your Spouse Comes Out
Published by The Haworth Press, Taylor & Francis Group, 2008. All rights reserved.
doi:10.1300/6046_06

lives to the disease. An estimated 38.6 million people across the world were living with HIV in 2005, with a resurgent epidemic in the United States and Europe among men who have sex with men (UNAIDS, 2006).

Since the HIV virus is often sexually transmitted, young adults are usually thought to be at greatest risk. However, the disease knows no age limits and it is dangerously naive to assume that older people are sexually inactive—even in a mature marriage. A 2004 AARP (formerly the American Association of Retired Persons) survey found that half of respondents aged forty-five plus reported that they were sexually active once a week or more, and 86 percent had engaged in sexual activities in the past six months (AARP, 2005).

Older people are increasingly facing AIDS, and the disease affects both men and women equally. By 2002, for the first time in the history of the epidemic, as many women as men were infected with HIV, according to UNAIDS (2006). In short, regardless of age or gender of straight partners, it is imperative for them to do as Emily did—go directly to a health clinic or doctor when a mate comes out. Testing may feel humiliating, but it can save your life!

Today's tests for HIV are highly accurate. The false-negative rate is less than one in a thousand. Formerly, test results weren't available for up to two weeks, but newer methods yield accurate results in just twenty minutes. A common apprehension is that the virus might "hide in your system," necessitating repeated tests for months or even years. AIDS authorities dispel this fear. Over 90 percent of infected people will test positive for HIV three months after exposure. At six months, 99.9 percent will test positive. At twelve months, it's 100 percent. It is therefore unnecessary to retest year after year, unless, of course, additional risk is assumed from new partners.

Besides such obvious risks as AIDS and various sexually transmitted diseases (STDs), other health issues for straight spouses should be recognized. Most of the interviewees experienced some trauma-induced sickness after their spouses' disclosure. Sandy had a chronic cough that persisted for months. Doctors couldn't diagnose its cause. She realized that it was a psychosomatic symptom only after she began to recover her emotional balance. Similarly, Beth suffered from severe laryngitis for two months after her gay lover left. It was a symbolic illness, for she had "lost her voice" emotionally, being unable to talk with anyone about her secret loss and pain. As a teacher, the laryngitis was totally debilitating, interfering with her work during that time. Beth finally consulted a counselor and spoke openly with close friends, *who got sick of hearing about it,* she recalls. With this outlet for her pent-up emotions, her disoriented, unsettled feelings began to subside and the laryngitis went away. Such emotion-induced illnesses are very common shortly after disclosure. Medical and psychological counsel is called for, along with the comfort of confidant(e)s.

These examples illustrate a finding of recent research. A University of California study found a physiological basis for social pain by monitoring the brains of people who thought others had maliciously excluded them (Eisenberger and Lieberman, 2003). They demonstrated that human pain centers register social rejection as well as physical pain. When we experience a loss, such as a death or the end of a love affair or marriage, shock and distress are registered in these pain centers. Mind, body, emotion, and spirit are all connected. The emotional jolt of a mate's homosexual disclosure often manifests as a physical ailment, such as Sandy's cough or Beth's laryngitis.

Long-term stress-related illnesses are even more stubborn and difficult to heal. Many interviewees reported suffering from such challenges as arthritis, high blood pressure, heart disease, and cancer. Four years after divorcing his lesbian wife, Charlie is recovering from heart surgery. Matt, whom we met in Chapter 1, also suffered a heart attack. While it is impossible to connect such infirmity directly with a single event, it is probable that stress over a long period of time contributes to its severity. The message from all these physical and psychological impacts is to seek competent professional help right away.

INEVITABLE ANGER

In Emily's case, and for many others, the realization of unrecognized long-term risk brought on the next great challenge: anger. Though anger is a natural, unavoidable occurrence in a straight spouse's recovery, it is also one of the most dangerous phases. Virtually everyone who experiences a mixed-orientation relationship feels rage in the midst of other stages of recovery. Usually, it comes again and again, often without warning, lessening in depth and duration as time passes.

Anger is often a secondary emotion, following hurt and fear. Anger itself is not bad or wrong; it is a normal reaction for straight spouses. It is how we <u>respond</u> to it that has the potential of further harm. Anger has little effect on its object—in this case, the homosexual partner. Rather, it is the angry person who suffers. A well-known Buddhist teacher, Pema Chödrön, suggests the apt analogy that harboring anger is like eating rat poison—and then expecting the rat to die.

Most of the straight spouses interviewed for this book spoke of episodes of rage. Lydia discovered that her husband of twenty-seven years had entertained a male lover in their home one weekend, while she visited her mother in a distant city. She was especially upset that one of their children was at home during the tryst. In fact, the child told her all about it. *They were in the bedroom all the time,* he reported.

The following month, Lydia's husband, Jonathan, discovered that his boyfriend was HIV positive. Jonathan rushed to the next city to be tested himself. Adding more misery to this fearful turn of events, Lydia was soon terminated from her church job, and three months later, Jonathan was fired from his public school teaching job. Not surprisingly, their junior-high-age twin sons became increasingly antisocial and troubled. Jonathan had betrayed his family, and he was increasingly harsh with their boys while coddling their daughter. Things got worse when Jonathan had their two sons "captured" and locked up in a mental hospital. He later sent them to a corrective boys' ranch to control their acting out. The household was chaotic.

These events were only examples of the hurt and disappointment Lydia experienced over several years. No wonder she felt rage, and she stayed deeply angry for a long time. Her blood pressure soared alarmingly. It was a dangerous state altogether. Persistent anger triples the risk of heart attack or sudden cardiac death. Its fight-or-flight response speeds the heart, raises blood pressure, and narrows the arteries. Repeated over time, these effects damage arteries and can trigger heart attack. Lydia's story is one example of the roots and effects of anger in a mixed-orientation situation. Such stories abound. The question is how to manage anger constructively, neither suppressing it entirely nor venting it aggressively. Either extreme is damaging.

Health authorities offer the following general suggestions to manage anger:

- Look deeply at the cause of the anger. Is it worthy of this focus? Can you let this incident go? Is this incident worth a fight?
- Use the "I messages" of *Nonviolent Communication* (Rosenberg, 2005). Describe your feelings and make a specific request: "I feel ____ when you do ____. I need ____. Would you be willing to do ____ instead?" This approach is better than the attack of "you messages": "You are ____ (bad). You make me furious." Others are more likely to respond when we offer information about our fundamental feelings and needs and the specific action that would be most helpful to us.
- Breathe deeply; consciously relax. Take up a meditation practice that is right for you.
- Exercise regularly and vigorously. Working the body helps clear the mind.
- Avoid depressants and stimulants. Alcohol loosens inhibitions and fuels anger; caffeine and nicotine intensify stress.
- Guard your general health with nourishing, regular meals, and sufficient, natural sleep. Avoid sleep aids or drugs.

Will these general suggestions rid us of all anger? Obviously not. But such wholesome approaches may help us regain balance. We seek the fine line between harmful overreaction and its opposite, suppression.

A THERAPEUTIC APPROACH TO ANGER

The fight response to fear, discussed in the last chapter, relates to anger. When we are threatened, strong feelings put the body into attack readiness. This body–mind state is recognized as the emotion of anger. We think, "I could rip his head off," or "I just want to choke her."

A subtler form of aggression turns back against the self in retroflection. Here, an individual's isolation becomes self-aggression, as internal energy fights against itself, instead of expressing itself outwardly. We may unconsciously suppress impulses that feel dangerous and forbidden. Anger then loops back against the self and suffocates life energy before we can consciously redirect it. This commonly translates into depression.

It is urgently important to address both conscious anger that is directed outwardly and unconscious, inwardly directed anger. Anger commonly follows fear and hurt as a defensive response. A wounded animal is as likely to bite a helping hand as a hurtful one. First, the animal is in a state of arousal and alert to further danger or attack. Second, the animal is protecting its wound from contact that could increase the pain of the initial injury. The emotional response of humans is not dissimilar. People commonly use anger and aggression for protection from further vulnerability and pain. If we are not in physical danger this response system tends to create additional problems, unless we learn to consciously redirect the energy to a constructive end.

To work with anger, the first step of awareness helps us see it precisely, without condemning ourselves for ensuing physical sensations or thoughts. Compassion in the midst of anger is essential, even if we have acted aggressively with regretful results. Ultimately, self-acceptance can melt anger in ways that self-control or self-punishment could not. To become more aware, accept the presence of anger and learn to breathe through its physical sensations and resultant thoughts. These thoughts build on themselves when we do not bring attention to them. Turning our witnessing function toward our anger rather than away from it paradoxically reduces its occurrence over time and reveals our vulnerability. This mindful approach helps prevent further self-aggression.

Insight follows in this process of working with rage and anger as we sort out our lives like the pieces of a puzzle that have been tossed in the air and have fallen helter-skelter. We come to understand that anger is workable as we sort our observations of bewildering feelings into piles of the different colored emotions—frustration, fear, grief, despair. We begin to understand why the anger occurs. When we suffer loss, feelings of anger arise to defend against the perception of greater loss around the corner. For example, feelings of anger point up injustice or mistreatment from our spouse. Recognition of present reality, which we may have been unable or unwilling to acknowledge in the past, can lead to more effective future decisions.

Utilizing the awareness of anger as a wake-up call does not mean we have to carry out an impulse to attack. Rather, it is essential to choose beneficial actions that work directly with rage. Regular physical release at the gym or on the trail can help, but at the height of emotion, overexercise can lead to injury. In that case, beating a pillow with an old tennis racket and yelling at the top of your lungs might be an effective but harmless way to express these boiling emotions in private. Writing a very angry letter that you will never send can also help you vent. Nothing is better than finding a trusted friend who will listen to your rage without judging it or provoking you to destructive actions. All of these approaches are helpful to contact and release these powerful emotions so they won't haunt you the rest of your life.

We are often afraid to express rage because the sadness lying below it seems overwhelming. Large feelings may be particularly scary because we haven't experienced them fully and do not trust that they naturally dissipate with time. Many individuals in crisis are afraid to unleash their anger or grief for fear of being swamped by these intense feelings. They are afraid that these drowning emotions will carry them away into insanity if they open the floodgates.

Actually, raging emotions eventually damage us if we do not contact them and consciously release their energy over time. After a huge, shocking loss these feelings continue to emerge much longer than we expect. Holding onto anger for years may be a sign that we have not surrendered to core feelings of vulnerability and grief hiding beneath the surface. Trying to get rid of deep emotions too fast just keeps them lingering indefinitely in the background, contaminating subsequent experiences, as we'll see in the next section.

1. Awareness of Anger
   - Observe the physical sensations that arise when you feel angry. Then focus internally, slow your breath by inhaling and exhaling fully, and notice any changes in your awareness.
   - Pay attention to the physical sensations of retroflection. Focus, slow your breath, and note any shifts in your awareness.
   - Examine any judgments you have toward sensations of anger, such as "I shouldn't feel this way." What changes when you let go of this thought, slow your breath, and focus on the physical sensations? Each time anger arises, repeat this simple exercise and see how the emotion dissipates over time with awareness and kindness toward your self.
2. Insight into Anger
   - Replace judgment with curiosity. Ask yourself, "Have I ever felt this angry before? When? What in my past makes anger so scary? What tools do I have to work with anger? How do I choose to work with anger now?"

- Observe when anger alerts you to injustice, abuse, or mis-treatment. Use your awareness to address situations that need to be corrected.
- Observe how anger is a label we attach to a combination of thoughts and bodily sensations. When else do you feel this much energy in your system? Imagine turning this energy into something positive for yourself or others.

3. Action Steps to Work with Anger

- Engage in regular physical exercise (not overdoing it at the height of rage).
- Find a location where you can vent anger by beating a pillow or yelling. Do not hurt yourself. You may discover grief be-neath your rage when you fully express yourself.
- Express your rage with someone in a letter you will never send. This may release feelings you can't directly express to the person. You will also be more capable of expressing your concerns rationally after verbally or physically venting pri-vately.
- Confide in someone who can accept your anger without judg-ment and without provoking you to destructive actions.

LOSS AND GRIEF

Emotionally, I have not recovered from the divorce, with the end-ing of all the dreams and companionship that entails. I feel all alone in the universe. Matt, whom we met in Chapter 1, clearly articulated this familiar theme for straight spouses—grief over the loss of future plans and sense of belonging. Grief is the other side of anger. One or the other may dominate in an individual, but both sides eventually need to be processed.

Grief was dominant over anger in Carol's experience. *I am not nat-urally an angry person. When Jim came out, my most memorable re-sponse was profound sadness. I described my grief as a black hole. Without warning, something would trigger my sadness and I'd stum-ble over the edge into that dark abyss. One way I kept my sanity in those first months of isolation was to keep a journal. Reading it today is like looking at old photographs. It evokes the depth of my familiar sorrow. I poured out my heart in passages like this: "Since this whole drama began, I have been afraid that if I ever let go of my tight hold on my emotions, if I ever start to weep, I might never stop crying. I've dammed up floods of tears. But I did let go last night. I cried bitterly all night. Everything I ever wanted is out of my grasp."*

Grief over layers of loss sometimes overwhelmed me, as this passage laments: *"Everything Jim and I have accomplished together no longer counts; our bright future plans will never be realized. Our business is gone. We will not enjoy a peaceful retirement together. We will not travel the world together. We will not know the security of mutual, loving support. We will not grow old together in our dear home. It's all gone."*

Sometimes Carol's grief alternated with the anger that it caused. On one occasion, while they were in the closet, still living together and trying to sell their business, Jim had taken yet another boating vacation with "the boys" at Lake Powell. Carol remembers, *I was buried in work at the office when he called from Bullfrog Marina to say he'd decided to stay there for a few more days—he was having such a good time. I was raw already, having just returned from a friend's funeral that had opened the wound of my own father's struggle with imminent death. Hearing Jim's jolly voice and laughter in the background salted the wound. I quietly hung up the phone and then exploded inside. I was furious that he was gaily entertaining himself while I lied to keep his secret and dutifully (if resentfully) kept home and business running. The unfairness made me crazy!* In those early days of her "knowing," the alternation of grief and anger often made Carol feel crazy.

In fact, all the emotions we feel tend to ebb and flow, come and go. Secrecy fosters fear and isolation, shame and self-doubt. Health risks often trigger anger. Many aspects of life in the closet are hooks for anger, which alternates with its partner, grief. As Claire said, it makes us feel "daffy." These personal emotions and challenges are experienced as early stages in the journey of a straight spouse. Suggestions for positive action are offered throughout this whole section of the book to aid the recovery process.

A THERAPEUTIC APPROACH TO GRIEF

Sadness, tears, and the need to slow down or come to a halt are all associated with loss. Most of us fight these necessary expressions because they are uncomfortable, run counter to our routine, and are not supported by a general trend in society to avoid grief. Dr. Elisabeth Kübler-Ross (1969), in her groundbreaking book *On Death and Dying*, points this out in her delineation of the stages of grief. Her outline is similar in many ways to the stages of coping of straight spouses, noted earlier (see Figure 3.1). The loss of a partner due to a different sexual orientation is the death of a marriage as it was known, negating years of trust and hopes tied to a lifetime commitment to fidelity. The straight partner's shock and both partners' disclosure challenges combine with the social stigma of homosexuality to create complicated grief (Kübler-Ross and Kessler, 2005). Complicated grief is defined by circumstances out of the normal range of experience, including multiple losses, traumatic circumstances, isolation, and polarized feelings toward the loved one, often exacerbated by a painful history together.

Even simple grief disrupts our customary habits, social roles, and defense mechanisms. Little support is available for time off in the workplace in most modern communities, where both parents work to maintain their home and family. A family in the throes of a coming-out crisis must somehow make space in normal routines to sit with sorrow, meeting the body's need to cry, sob, rest, and recover from this deathlike loss. Kübler-Ross's research on grief offers signposts for straight spouse coping strategies that encourage progress toward healing.

The first stage of grief is denial. It is often accompanied by such thoughts as "It's not true" or "I can't believe this is happening to me." Some people behave as if nothing has changed; others try to lose themselves in increased activity that signals deflection. Prolonged denial can lead to debilitating addiction or regression in severe circumstances. Consciously bringing our attention to the present moment and our bodily sensations helps us return to reality when we are in denial. The commitment to live one day at a time can help us stay grounded, protecting us from exaggerated fear of the future that sends us into flight.

In the second stage of anger, fight behaviors arise in angry thoughts. Aggression toward our partner, others, or our own self is a futile attempt to recover losses. Our minds look for a cause and someone to punish or blame. While it is important to take the necessary time to work through anger and hurt, without denying these feelings, prolonged clinging to resentment eventually corrodes confidence in self-determination. While we can't control outer circumstances, we are capable of seeing what we can change, including our attitude toward this painful loss.

The third stage is bargaining and wishful thinking. "If I become the perfect spouse, my partner will change." "If I make a promise to God, my spouse will become straight." "If I give up my desire for sex and romance, we can live happily ever after." Such statements characterize bargaining. We can go through life stuck in a future fantasy and never realize intimacy because we are hoping for it to come from someone who is not available to us. In becoming aware of this process, it is helpful to be gentle with our wishful thinking, realizing that it comes from a deeper need for love shared by all humankind. Trusting that companionship and love are eventually possible requires optimism that may seem out of reach. Many find that seeking guidance through inspirational books, lectures, and shared stories of recovery helps them remember that renewal is achievable.

Few people escape the fourth stage of depression in the grief process. Enormous energy is tied up in putting a lid on sadness, and the internal pressure can feel intense and confusing. Depression is like a great weight on top of this lid that translates into loss of energy, poor self-care, spiraling negative thoughts, hopelessness, and defeat. Somatic symptoms can show up in interrupted sleep patterns, loss of appetite, and forgetfulness. Simply maintaining normal function takes monumental effort. Individuals who are biologically prone to clinical depression and those who experience severe symptoms should seek additional medical and/or psychological assistance.

Weathering depression for most people is facilitated by allowing time and space for sadness to surface and release. Many people confuse the body's physical response to grief as depression and fight it by suppressing expressions of sorrow. This attempt typically backfires and depression actually increases. If we gradually allow the pressure valve to open a little at first and then incrementally more as sensations of grief become normalized, we may slowly release our dammed-up feelings. While this gradual process is ideal, it may not always be possible. Again, nothing works better than sharing tears with a trusted confidant(e) who can help allay our fears of drowning when the floodgates open. The fact that grief is a normal response to loss cannot be overemphasized. Remember this when taking time to reflect on sadness or cry alone.

Acceptance is the final stage in the grief process and is fostered again through the three-step healing practice of awareness, insight, and action. Awareness of these stages heightens self-understanding and facilitates the process. One may experience the stages of grief in a different order, lean into some more than others, or experience them simultaneously. Our inner witness, nurtured through continued observation of these stages, becomes an ally on the journey, as we develop patience and a nonjudgmental attitude.

Insight develops into a compassionate view, not an overly critical analysis of inner defenses and outer problems. Action follows, carving out time, creating a comfortable space to grieve, and seeking others who kindly share our sorrow and tears. Designing a simple ritual to represent our bereavement and release of the past may help us complete this stage. The following healing practices may also serve as steps toward acceptance of loss. Marks of acceptance are increased peace of mind, enjoyment, and reinvestment in new life.

1. Awareness of Grief
   • Recognize the stages of grief:
     —Denial
     —Anger
     —Bargaining
     —Depression
     —Acceptance
   • Develop an inner witness to these stages through continued observation and identification of the signs of each stage. Notice the order of the stages in your experience. Which stage is most difficult or persistent? Which do you try to avoid?
2. Insight into Grief
   • Observe if your grief is complicated by factors other than a mixed-orientation marriage:
     —Circumstances out of the normal range of experience
     —Multiple losses
     —Trauma
     —Isolation
     —Polarized feelings toward the loved one (often due to a painful history together)

- Develop your insight into a compassionate view. Note whether your analysis of the stages of grief reflects a cynical or defeatist attitude. Reverse this process by reviewing the material and returning to the awareness phase.
- Reflect on grief as a natural process. Remember that all change involves loss and requires a degree of letting go before life can begin anew.

3. Actions to Complete Grief
    - Recognize any denial and commit to living one day at a time.
    - Take time to process anger and resentment, as directed previously in this chapter.
    - Stop bargaining by looking for real solutions. Seek guidance in inspirational books, lectures, and shared stories of recovery.
    - Give yourself time, space, and companionship through the period of depression. Allow emotional, verbal, and physical expression of grief.
    - Commemorate your acceptance of loss and release the past through a ritual, activity, or ceremony. Private or shared events can help mark the beginning of a new life. You might consider a journey, spiritual retreat, gathering of the people who have supported you, or an expression in poetry, art, music, or dance.

These last two chapters have examined several major challenges that straight spouses face personally. The highlighted obstacles are among the first encountered after a gay mate's disclosure. But gay–straight relationships affect entire families and social circles. The next chapter explores those wider issues.

QUESTIONS TO PONDER

1. What am I most afraid of right now?
2. What am I most angry about?
3. What is my greatest loss?
4. What threatens me most about this?
5. What can I do right now to cope with these emotions?

ACTIVITIES

1. In your journal, write your answers to the "Questions to Ponder," focusing on what you can do now to move forward. Writing is similar to confession in its healing power. Capturing confusion in words on paper creates some sense of order and makes the situation less threatening.
2. If you haven't already done so, make an appointment with a health care center for an AIDS test and information on safe sex. Protect yourself!
3. Try this meditative exercise: Visualize yourself one year from today. Imagine yourself in a calm and peaceful state with the present pain gone. See yourself healed. Repeat this exercise whenever you feel discouraged.

Chapter 7

Family and Social Challenges

Most of the chapters in this book focus on the recovery of the straight spouse. But it's obvious that a mate's coming out dramatically impacts the entire family, both nuclear and extended. Moreover, the couple's unfolding drama also affects their social circle. Sometimes those effects are subtle, almost covert; sometimes friendships simply disappear. This chapter addresses some of the major family and social issues that must be faced when a spouse comes out, particularly the pressing priority of the couple's children. Several examples of these relationship issues will be followed by analysis and concrete suggestions for positive action.

TELLING THE CHILDREN

If there are children in the family when a spouse comes out, some immediate decisions must be made: if, when, and how to tell them the truth; how much to tell and how soon.

How can young people understand such a complex issue? Their age, maturity, and general stability all affect the answer to this question. Many experts suggest explaining the situation in stages, not overwhelming the child with too much information at once. It is also important to use language the young person can understand, being careful not to malign the gay partner. Divisive behavior and hateful words inevitably wound the child even further and damage future family relationships. Individual situations obviously vary, so parents must forge their own methods and find their own words. However, a few good examples may offer some guidance.

When Sharon came out to him, Matt did a sensitive job of explaining imminent changes in their household to their four-year-old son,

When Your Spouse Comes Out
Published by The Haworth Press, Taylor & Francis Group, 2008. All rights reserved.
doi:10.1300/6046_07

Danny. Sharon was still in the closet and the three of them were still together in their home. When Matt moved into a separate bedroom, Danny needed an explanation. Matt began by saying that there were going to be some changes. *Mommy has realized that she is what's called "gay." (I didn't use the word "lesbian.") Most people, men and women, like and want to live together as husband and wife, but with gay people, men like men and women like women and that's who they want to be partners with for their life. There isn't anything wrong with it. It's just like people have different hair colors and skin colors, different heights—some people are taller and some people are shorter. While most people aren't that way, there are a lot of people who are gay. Your mommy has figured out that she is one of those people. At some point, it will mean that Mommy and I won't be married anymore. But we'll both still be your parents and it doesn't change how we love you. This isn't your fault. It isn't anything you have done. For the time being, things will stay the same here at home.*

Notice the language level for a small child and reinforced reassurance that Danny would still have two loving parents and that the immediate changes would not threaten him—and weren't his fault. These points are important to make, regardless of the age of the child. Sharon came out publicly a year later and she and Matt were officially divorced after that. Danny seems to have weathered the transition and is presently thriving in junior high.

Explaining to older children presents a different challenge. Carlotta and David had a son and daughter who were thirteen and eighteen when David disclosed his homosexuality to his wife. Though this couple immediately realized that their marriage would end, their family still existed as a high priority. Their focus was to preserve family ties in some form. Carlotta needed time to process her new knowledge and its implications. She spent six months doing so. When the time seemed right, they called a family meeting and told the whole truth to their teenagers, answering all questions honestly. These caring parents' months of private discussion, reading, and adjustment prepared them well. Both teens discreetly told their friends and had immediate peer support. They also adjusted to the changes, knowing that both parents were behind them. They went on to college and are launching successful lives of their own now.

Waiting until the heat of the discovery has cooled is a good idea. Carlotta gave herself time to recover from her own shock, worked through her immediate personal issues, and prepared herself to support her children through their time of recovery. Straight talk to older children is important. Telling the truth is better than holding back, unless there is some compelling reason to do so.

If the children are older at the time a parent comes out, disclosure may be less difficult. When Bonnie and Stan decided to divorce, after both had protected Stan's secret for many years, they devised an unusual plan to tell family and friends. They arranged a gathering of their whole family and a separate meeting of their closest friends. There, they read letters they each had composed to explain their situation and their personal feelings. After they read their letters, they offered to answer any questions. Then they left, allowing space and time for their surprised loved ones to talk and begin to process their unexpected news.

Jim and Carol also went together to tell each member of their families—his mother in Colorado, one son in California, and Carol's mother, along with their other son and his wife in Tulsa. Carol recommends such openness: *First, we told them that we were about to separate, and then we told them why. If we hadn't shared the whole truth, they never could have understood why our thirty-plus-year marriage was ending. Telling the truth freed us all to help each other reach acceptance.*

Truth binds. Secrecy separates. Kaye, whose story was told in Chapter 2, suffered greatly from her daughter's simmering anger about the family's long-term secret. Kaye took harsh blame for not telling her daughter about Joseph's homosexuality much sooner. Similarly, Kim's children also blamed their mother for harboring her husband's secret. These examples suggest openness with children at the earliest opportunity, regardless of their age.

Truth also frees. Sarah recounted a scene she'll always carry in her memory. *The morning following our decision to let each other go was like this: Although we realized what a heart- and life-wrenching decision we had made, we went for a bike ride with our son along the dirt roads of some property we had in the mountains. My husband rode his bike like a kid who'd just learned to ride alone without training wheels. He told me later he was feeling as if he'd just dropped a burden, a terrible burden he'd carried for years—not the burden of our marriage but the burden of hidden truth of who he was. In a similar* way, all the members of a mixed-orientation family can feel liberated when their secret is out.

CO-PARENTING AND SINGLE PARENTING

When one of the partners discloses homosexuality, most couples decide to separate, and roughly two-thirds of these mixed-orientation marriages eventually end in divorce (PFLAG, 2006). Those who are parents, especially with younger children, must manage a more complicated situation than childless couples.

If the separation is relatively peaceful, co-parenting is a possibility. Matt and Sharon, for example, still move their son Danny between their households every weekend. Since they live near each other, and since they try hard to make each house a real home for the boy, the weekly exchange has worked for them. The downside for Matt is that he has invested so much energy into making Danny comfortable that he has not fulfilled his own need to reconstruct his life or develop a new relationship.

Lee and Randy have achieved better balance between their roles as divorced parents and their needs as single adults. Lee is a focused, self-directed straight spouse who feels good about sharing parenting with her ex-husband. *My ex and I are very flexible about the time we spend with our daughter. We trade off nights and weekends. My daughter is a well-adjusted child of divorce, according to her third-grade teacher. I think that is due to the fact that Randy and I don't fight over her—or over anything. We work things out and both have a willingness to see that things are smooth among all of us.*

Lee achieved this smoothness partly through her own recovery from the stresses of her eleven-year marriage, during which she knew about Randy's sexual orientation. He actually told her during their honeymoon! They intentionally decided to stay together anyway. Keeping his secret was a great hardship, however. *I lived my life as a big lie for a very long time. I was shoved into the closet with him, not by my own choosing. Currently, the most important thing to me is honesty.*

When Randy finally decided to come out entirely, partly through the encouragement of a support group of formerly married gay men, Lee knew that she would have to be stronger than ever before. *One thing that helped me through the divorce part of this process was that*

I decided what my goals were. I wanted my daughter, my dog, and my retirement. I wanted to be living in my own house, the house that I chose. I kept my eyes on these goals; anything else was just a little bump in the road. If it didn't effect my goals, it got very little attention. I was able to fix my eyesight on my future and where I wanted to be.

Lee achieved her goals, buying her own home and presently living there with her daughter and two pet dogs. She has a rewarding job as a computer professional with an education-related government agency. She's confident and happy again in a new relationship. Despite inevitable alienation at the time of their separation, the strain between Lee and Randy eased. *My ex and I have a friendship now that revolves around our daughter. Sometimes, the three of us even go camping together. I still go to a lot of Randy's family gatherings, and my family has finally accepted what has happened and how we are proceeding as friends. But Randy has gone on with his life and I have gone on with mine. Our daughter is happier now because her parents are happier. She sees the shared time with us as "not a big deal," so I think she's well-adjusted.*

Carlotta and David, who were mentioned in the previous section, also co-parented their two teenagers. The kids became as comfortable at home with their father and his gay partner as they were in their mother's house. Family ties are extremely important in their Hispanic culture. Despite their divorce, Carlotta and David were willing to work hard to maintain civility and cohesiveness. Carlotta used the same technique that Lee mentioned: visualization. Both women talked of visualizing a happy future, using their mental images to guide their daily actions. Carlotta, for example, holds a Thanksgiving dinner image. *Ten years from now, I see the kids and David and me together at the table—all still friends, all happy with new partners.*

Co-parenting worked in these examples, but it isn't always possible. Sandy and James don't enjoy the same respectful friendship. Instead, Sandy maintains strong boundaries. *I have tried various ways to interact with him for the sake of our child but have found that, for my own mental health and emotional stability, the less I have to do with him the better. I don't get sucked into draining melodramas with him, as long as my interactions with him are exclusively about Erin and don't involve money. If we are in the same place at the same time, merely as observers of a play or performance by our daughter, things work just fine. But the moment the boundaries are lowered to include other events, it seems that I regret it, emotionally or monetarily, or both. Recently, I have been able to afford to pay for Erin's needs and wants without asking him to share the cost. What I spend in money, I believe I am banking in emotional stability.*

While she wishes it were otherwise, Sandy has taken the whole responsibility for Erin's upbringing. *Ideally, Erin would have two parents who get along beautifully and give and take in the responsibility of raising her. Since that is not possible, I believe it is healthier for her and me if her dad and I are at least not fighting.* After a pause to consider the meaning of all this, Sandy concluded, *I believe it is better for the mental health of both my ex-husband and myself if we maintain a businesslike distance from each other. When we interact too much, it is toxic for both of us.*

The result is that Sandy considers herself an independent single parent. *My immediate family consists of my daughter and myself. I am envious of those who have been able to include ex-spouses and their partners within the family circle. That has not been possible for me, and I know that has an impact on Erin.* But Sandy also notes some good news: *On the plus side, having a gay dad has made my daughter tolerant and accepting of people who are different. Her friends are quite clear that she will stand up for and with them if there is ever a need.*

Sandy enjoys her close ties with her daughter and also feels proud of her own growth as a person. *Erin and I have a great relationship. We do a lot together and enjoy each other's company. I try to be encouraging without being pushy, and supportive without expecting perfection. The teen years are fast approaching, but I feel confident we have established a solid base. She is very fashion oriented, often helping choose outfits for me to wear on dates. Last week, she even did a makeover on me. (I must say, I looked pretty good.)* Asked to describe her current feelings about James, she thought for a moment and said, *I have grown as a result of knowing him. Also, I have grown as a result of leaving him.*

How divorced couples share parenting responsibilities is highly individual, depending on both external and internal factors. One of those factors is their success in dealing with anger. It is worth noting that all of these divorced straight spouses experienced their inevitable stage of anger. Everyone does. Anger manifested mostly as depression for Matt and Lee. It showed up as recurring rage for Sandy. All have made progress from the depth of their pain, though their resentment occasionally resurfaces. Their subsequent ability to co-parent has an obvious relation to their skill in managing their anger. Other variables range from overall emotional stability to financial means to physical proximity. However, when the welfare of the child is foremost, the outcome is more hopeful for all. The next case study illustrates this truth, as we see how one father dramatically knit the frayed edges of his torn family back together.

RE-CREATING FAMILY

Mark and Lisa had been married fifteen years with an eleven-year-old son and a seven-year-old daughter when Lisa began to self-identify as a lesbian. *My wife was very open about her awakening. She told me one day that she and her best friend, who was also married, had suddenly found themselves kissing each other. Months later, after much deliberation, she informed me that she felt she needed to consummate her attraction for her friend by becoming lovers. Soon after she slept with her friend, she told me what had happened, though not in detail. It took at least a year from that point before she acknowledged that she had somehow "changed" or awakened to her current sexual orientation.*

What Mark didn't know was that Lisa had a secret, ongoing affair with her friend during that year. When she did tell Mark the truth, he was livid: *That wasn't our agreement! After Lisa and her friend became lovers, I told her that I couldn't continue in our marriage if she continued her affair.* The couple struggled for some months after that. *It was a very disturbing time.* Confused and troubled, they spent months in joint counseling. Lisa said at the time that she wanted their marriage to be her top priority.

Still, Mark worried about Lisa's clandestine relationship during those months of counseling. *Although the two women were not physically lovers, their connection was threatening and strong. Her friend decided to leave her marriage; Lisa stuck with ours and we continued counseling. We talked about alternative marriage contracts, an "open marriage," finding some way for her to feel she could find expression for what she was calling her "lesbian self" without ending our marriage. We talked about setting up a separate bedroom so she could have a room of her own for part of the time. But essentially, we continued with our basic marriage contract regarding monogamy. I needed to be my wife's primary relationship.*

During this year of turmoil, the children *did not consciously know, although they certainly could feel some of the tension between us, and noticed that Lisa and her friend were especially close.* (It is interesting that Lisa's realization of her lesbian identity followed a similar revelation by her sister, who also came out after rearing two children almost to adulthood.) Finally, Mark's attempts to keep the marriage intact failed. Lisa made her choice and took the next step.

Though she had a master's degree and was trained as a teacher, she enrolled in an alternative school in Oregon to study psychotherapy. There, she found a new lover. *Before we separated, she got into a relationship with another woman who lived a thousand miles away. She intended to move to be with her new partner in Portland and was open about that to everyone. We told our kids, and Lisa pretty quickly began self-identifying as a lesbian quite openly. My greatest fear had been that she would decide that because of her need/desire to be in relationship with women, she would leave our marriage. I never even thought about the possibility of her leaving the children as well.*

When Lisa told me she was moving out of state and I would be raising the children by myself, I was incredulous and incredibly upset. I am still baffled by the sequence of events, still feel like I do not understand what exactly happened with her. I know many women (and men) who have learned/accepted/come out with their homosexuality late in life, but that doesn't explain why she was willing to also deny her motherhood. I am upset at her because she has disengaged so much from the kids and am still very sad that the woman I loved and intended to spend my life with decided to leave.

What do you do in a situation like this? Mark was suddenly the sole parent for his two children, faced with the necessity to reconstruct their family of three. Adding to the burden of being both mother and father, he also had to change his career path. He had built a successful reputation as a journalist, working for a major weekly news magazine and traveling extensively on assignment. Now he would be housebound, fulfilling the roles of mother and father and sole breadwinner. He was understandably overwhelmed when he quit his secure job and became a freelance writer, working at home.

One kind of turning point came when I realized that I was getting much closer to my kids. It might have been something as simple as

*baking brownies with my daughter to take to a school fund-raiser. An-
other marker was when my wife moved away permanently, and I realized that nothing was going to change, and this was indeed what my
new life was going to look like. Our divorce paled in intensity in many
ways to the fact that she left the state.*

One year to the day after their divorce was final, Mark suffered another personal loss when his dearly loved brother died of breast cancer. *Losing him in many ways was so much worse, so much more final
than Lisa's change of sexual orientation or even the end of our marriage. It also put my grief into a deeper, lonelier spot, and I felt overwhelmed at the quantity of loss I had endured over such a short
period of time.*

Rather than let his grief and sadness engulf him, Mark conceived a
creative plan. *With my life in unconditional disarray, I chose to em-
bark on my odyssey into single fatherhood in an admittedly unusual
way: By taking my kids to python-infested jungles in Borneo searching for wild orangutans; into remote mountains in Vietnam tracking
Javan rhinos; and to the northern edge of the Gangeatic plains stalk-
ing Bengal tigers. I wanted to show my son and daughter this planet's
amazing animals and extraordinary landscapes.* During six months
of travel in these exotic places, Mark hoped to re-create his little family and reinforce their bonds. He wanted to seek out these endangered
animals and share the experience with his children—before they also
were gone. *Perhaps, I thought, we could forge a new family of three,
using adventure as our crucible. We did and lived to tell about it.*

Mark now sees his single parenthood as a blessing. *It didn't take
me long to realize what a gift it is to raise these kids. I'm totally involved. It's wonderful.* Admittedly, Mark's method of dealing with a
new family dynamic is unusual, but it worked. *Our trip around the
world established the three of us as an adventurous trio, even minus
Mom. Mostly though, time is doing its healing work.* Mark's best advice is, *Don't push the river.* Regardless of the method, the goal is to
heal the wounds in the family and draw it back together through mutual support and effort. How does one begin? It helps to understand
how children view the world at different ages.

DEVELOPMENTAL CHALLENGES WITH CHILDREN

Children at different ages and stages of development have very diverse needs when family structure changes. Most of the professional advice for families experiencing divorce also applies to children of mixed-orientation parents. The needs of young children revolve primarily around safety. Gradual change over time helps them absorb the losses that change entails. Many older children respond to family disruption with a complicated form of grief that requires extra time and attention from adults. Children and adolescents who are old enough to feel negative peer or community attitudes toward homosexuality particularly need support as they negotiate their own identity formation and developing role in society. In this section, we'll examine parental attitudes and actions that support children through the upheavals that coming out, separation, and changing family memberships may elicit.

Nothing is more important than looking at the needs of your child through their eyes. It is crucial to remember that the parents' central concerns do not match the child's concerns. Working as a team, educating yourselves as parents, and developing a thoughtful strategy will greatly impact your child's long-term well-being. This task is formidable for parents at the height of emotional distress and marital difficulty. But focusing on the children may help stabilize the parents as well.

The unfamiliar or shocking nature of your situation may prompt an abrupt decision to separate. The gay spouse may want to make immediate changes after living for years in the closet, or the straight spouse may want an immediate divorce. It is important to resist the impulse to rush, and instead to make reasoned, adult decisions that consider the family unit as a whole, as Carlotta and David did in a previous example. Even if one partner is unwilling to work as a team member, it is still important to maintain the integrity of his or her parenthood in your child's eyes.

A child's age influences the shape of the process. To an infant, love means comfort, food, and nourishment of all the senses, including touch, movement, sight, and sound (Heller, 1997). Caring for a newborn or infant is a time-consuming and emotionally demanding responsibility for any parent. For a very anxious or depressed parent, these basic tasks can be overwhelming. Assistance of family, friends, and child care facilities may be necessary when the parent's capacity is challenged.

Children between the ages of two and five equate love with spending time together. It is most important to assure them of a consistent environment. Make changes slowly to give these children time to understand that new households or additional family members do not mean competition or less love for them. To them, their parents' sexual orientation is not the primary concern. It is not always essential to share this information unless a serious gay partner is brought into the picture as a potential family member. Older children in this age range may need simple explanations of "gay," "lesbian," or "homosexual"—words they may hear among peers or relatives.

Needs of children ages five to ten are similar to those of younger children, though their love equation is more complex. They are beginning to model their behavior after adults in more conscious ways and the acceptance of their peer group is essential. A family separation or stigmatized parent can mean a loss in their sense of self-worth and belonging in the world. Assurance of love means continued activities with both parents. While they may wonder why parents are separating, coming out to children this age is only pertinent if concrete events, such as a same-sex partnership or talk in the community, impact them directly. If possible, it is best to help them through one major adjustment at a time.

Children between five and ten years old develop most of their sense of right and wrong through rules and observing others (Erikson, 1950). They may be very sensitive to the dominant standards expressed in their neighborhood, particularly if there are negative attitudes toward homosexuality. Living with the knowledge of a gay parent's sexual orientation as an abstraction without an outer context is likely to be confusing and isolating. Experiencing the parent in a loving gay relationship is a context that can promote understanding and acceptance of this new reality.

Adolescence is a tenuous time even when parental relationships are healthy (Erikson, 1968). Adjusting to a gay parent's orientation adds complexity. It is most difficult for teens if they experience internal judgment toward homosexuality or encounter homophobic attitudes from their peers or social milieu. These pressures exaggerate teenagers' fears when their parents divorce or choose new partners. One of their major developmental tasks is self-determination and emancipation from the family unit. When this unit is shaken, it becomes even harder for them to determine their needs and identity separate from others. Their task of identity formation involves understanding personal strengths and limitations. They need a stable home to push against to successfully launch into the world. It is therefore essential for parents to provide stability even in times of crisis. Witnessing parents' ability to cope under stress positively impacts youngsters' belief in their ability to survive through painful circumstances.

Adolescents are also forming their own sexual role as a developmental task. This development evokes feelings of insecurity, making teens very sensitive to others' judgments. They have a growing need for privacy that can make them hard to reach. While teens appreciate honesty, it is not helpful to share details about parents' sexual interests and behavior. Young adolescents are often repulsed by any thought of their parents' sexuality as they begin to wrestle with their own developing sexual feelings. Older teens may have an easier time understanding the logic of a parent's coming out and feel less vulnerable to being judged by others for a parent's actions. Emphasizing that sexuality is just one aspect of a loving adult relationship helps adolescents adjust to their changing circumstances. Consistent modeling of love and acceptance by all the adults involved helps young people at any age accept family changes.

The discovery of their unique gift and contribution to the world is the final task of adolescent development. It is imperative to maintain the integrity of the parental role. A strong home base protects youngsters from being overwhelmed by parental problems or, worse, drifting away from the family as a central place to derive values and recognition. Their sense of effectiveness is challenged when they experience the same outer limitations and judgments that are placed on a stigmatized family member. Learning how to work with differences develops compassion and inner strength that does not require outer approval. Children discover their uniqueness and life path by being supported in their experimental quests until they are ready to fly on their own. Despite the losses your child may be experiencing, consistent parenting means maintaining the same limits and opportunities previously set.

Divorce or the revelation of a parent's homosexual identity may elicit a variety of emotional reactions from children, regardless of their age. Children in denial and silence may be defending themselves against disruptions they find overwhelming. Parents may misinterpret this reaction as acceptance of the situation. Regressive behaviors are not uncommon for anxious children trying to manage threats to their familiar world. Physical complaints may increase as youngsters generalize their fears of loss to basic needs for food, shelter, and bodily safety, or they may commit hostile acts when they fail to manage their frustration or feelings of guilt.

Young children commonly believe they have caused their parents' problems. Preschoolers may believe they created their parents' breakup because of magical thinking at this age. Teens can be obsessed with guilt or shame when they have no outlets for their feelings. Any of these behaviors may occur at a time of loss or significant change. These responses become problematic when they last over time or increase in intensity. Helping children and adolescents understand that a loss or change in the family is not their fault is critical at any age.

While many children are resilient and creative in finding ways of coping with change, providing opportunities for conversation and the expression of feelings is of utmost importance. Such exchanges help them cope successfully with the stress of divorce or homophobic community attitudes. Young children can be encouraged to express their feelings through play activities and enactments with dolls, stuffed animals, fantasy activities, or art materials. A child therapist may be needed if emotional reactions are prolonged and difficult. A family therapist may facilitate communication with children and adolescents if it becomes obvious that isolation or acting out is affecting their home, learning, or social functioning.

Several books are available for children and adolescents that can help normalize their experience. *How It Feels to Have a Gay or Lesbian Parent: A Book by Kids for Kids of All Ages,* by Judith Snow (2004), is an excellent resource. Abigail Garner's (2005) *Families Like Mine: Children of Gay Parents Tell It Like It Is* offers a great resource for both adolescents and parents. Numerous children's books on divorce and separation are available for preschoolers and elementary age kids. Books for adults on co-parenting and helping children cope with divorce are also available and listed in the resource section at the end of this book. Remember, you do not have to reinvent the wheel; much of the literature on these topics is full of insight, good advice, and helpful tips.

Developmental stages are not fixed, and variations exist even among children in the same family. In fortunate communities where the outlook is less judgmental toward homosexuality, children are exposed to more tolerant attitudes early in their development. Regardless of the outer environment, however, it is essential that parents educate themselves about the particulars of their children's inner feelings and the social world they inhabit. Homophobic attitudes that are not obvious can greatly impact a child's experience. The general guidelines offered here may assist parents to adjust their methods creatively to meet this family-wide crisis.

UNDERSTANDING YOUR GAY PARTNER'S PROCESS

Helping children adjust during this upheaval is a primary priority, but it is also important to understand the gay partner's evolution of self-recognition. Understanding the psychological process helps straight spouses feel less disoriented and better able to cope with unexpected and puzzling behaviors. Your ability to relate to your gay spouse is greatly influenced by the stage of your spouse's homosexual identity formation (Cass, 1979). Vivienne Cass developed this theoretical model after years of research and working with homosexual individuals and interpersonal dynamics (Cass, 1984). It's important to remember that your gay spouse's pattern of change does not reflect on your capacity as a wife or husband. Instead, there is usually a long period of internal wrestling with the question of sexual identity before most homosexuals come out. Cass's model demonstrates why. From this six-stage formulation we can deduce why even people closest to married gays are left in the dark for so long and so shocked by their coming out.

The first stage of identity confusion begins with the awareness of thoughts, feelings, and behaviors that are experienced as incongruent to one's heterosexual identity. Inner turmoil and alienation mark this stage, while the individual attempts to resolve sexual confusion in isolation. Two outcomes are likely in this phase: Inhibition and denial may bring foreclosure to the issue, or continued stresses of the incongruent homosexual manifestations push the individual into the next stage of identity comparison.

In this second stage, individuals are sharply aware of comparing themselves with others and noting how they are different. The feeling of not belonging is a common expression of social alienation and some individuals may seek counseling at this time. Not wanting to be "different" is a generally expressed concern and they will most likely continue to pass as heterosexual. Some may feel good about their growing awareness of homosexuality, while others try to inhibit it through denial, greater heterosexual behavior, or by becoming asexual. Many will devalue themselves and begin a pattern of self-hatred that in extreme forms can lead to suicide.

The tensions of that second stage can lead to identity tolerance when individuals conceive of themselves as probably gay and begin seeking contact with the homosexual subculture. As feelings of isolation and alienation from homosexuality decrease, they begin to detach emotionally from heterosexual relationships. Their straight spouses may notice emotional distance. During this phase, any negative experiences with gay individuals typically feed self-hatred and lead to the wish to end homosexual desires. In contrast, if contacts with gay or lesbian individuals feel positive, less helplessness and greater self-esteem may result. Anxiety over possible discovery of their new activities can intensify as contact with the homosexual community increases.

In the fourth stage of identity acceptance, identification with other homosexuals increases. They may selectively disclose their identity to heterosexuals who are willing to keep their secret. While they manage to fit in with both gay and straight culture, inner conflict between their gay identity and society's rejection may lead to the next, more outwardly active stance.

Identity pride increases valuation of homosexual culture and decreases valuation of heterosexual norms. Anger about real societal limitations of their newly revealed status is commonly experienced at this stage. Gay individuals are likely to alter their job, marriage, or home while deepening their commitment to the gay community in this phase. Changing attitudes may be expressed destructively in impulsive actions or constructively in activism on gay issues such as AIDS.

Positive contacts and acceptance from members of the heterosexual community may tip the scales toward the sixth stage of identity synthesis. Anger and pride may still exist, but they are tempered as the gay person experiences similarities to straight individuals and dissimilarities to other homosexuals. Gaining broader perspective, the person integrates the gay identity as one among other important aspects of the self. Personal and public identities are synthesized when there is strong support in both gay and straight personal relationships.

This whole process of gay self-identification deeply impacts family and close associates. During the first stages of <u>identity confusion</u> and <u>comparison</u> you may experience your gay partner as emotionally suppressed, distant, depressed, needy, or alternating between neediness and emotional distance. In <u>identity tolerance</u> and <u>acceptance</u> your partner may be more confident, but also more detached. Increased absences mark greater involvement with the homosexual community. Your mate's life is split between two worlds, putting you both in the closet.

In the <u>identity pride</u> phase, your partner may make dramatic, impulsive, or abrupt changes, swinging to the pole of a gay lifestyle. Straight partners usually experience rejection that has little to do with them personally. But if the gay mate moves on to the final stage of <u>identity synthesis</u>, the couple may develop a more balanced, friendly relationship.

No individual fits perfectly into a theoretical model and variations are common, including partners who identify as bisexual or become transgendered. But the outline described here should clarify confusing changes in your partnership and shed light on the foregoing examples. A perplexed, highly conflicted individual may remain undecided in his or her sexual identity for many years. Discrimination against sexual minorities is a strong factor that impacts your partner and your marriage. If your spouse is open to discussion of it, sharing this model might begin a dialogue to help both of you ease tension and gain perspective.

RELATING TO A GAY MATE

"To stay, or not to stay? And if we separate, how will we feel about each other? Can we relate at all?" These are fundamental questions every straight spouse must answer. Most mixed couples eventually do divorce, but regardless of that decision, the fact remains that some contact between them will continue—particularly if they have children. Divorced or together, in or out of the closet, some connection usually remains. How will it look?

We have already seen a variety of examples. Kaye and Joseph continue their marriage, relating to each other as friends and companions. Matt and Sharon are held together only by their son, Danny. Their contact is strained by Sharon's inexplicable, enduring anger toward Matt. Bonnie and Stan are friendly but have infrequent visits, and Bonnie has remarried and created an entirely new life in a different state. Jim and Carol also live hundreds of miles apart, but their children and grandchildren and shared responsibility for his aged mother keep them in contact. Carol is grateful that their relationship is warm: *To me, Jim now seems like an old friend or a distant relative.* These are some of the scenarios one might expect as years pass after a gay spouse comes out. Life continues.

The shape of these later relationships is greatly affected by the closeness of the couple's ties before a mate comes out and by the tenor of the homosexual disclosure. If it is abrupt and hostile, there is little chance for friendly connection later. If there is shocking discovery of homosexual activity, like Kim's or Lydia's, there is even less optimism. Surprising your husband in your bedroom with his male lover isn't conducive to a warm, fuzzy outcome! Regardless of the beginning circumstances, however, it is worthwhile to make a genuine effort to stay friendly, particularly if there are children from the union. A number of positive role models emerged through the interviews that offer patterns for a healthy later connection, proving that it is possible and worthy of effort.

Over and over, the phrase "time heals" was heard in interviews of straight spouses who were several years past their mates' coming out. It is a cliché because it's true. The bleeding stops, the open wounds close, and the scars that remain become less noticeable. A point made in the co-parenting section also applies here. If the dark pit of anger and depression can be experienced and passed through successfully, forgiveness and release are possible. One example is that Lee and Randy can now take their daughter camping—as friends.

Sarah is another excellent role model for relating to an ex. Again, the tincture of time helped. Twenty years have passed since Tim, Sarah's husband, came out. Sarah later married a longtime friend of the family and describes herself now as *usually confident, cheerful, eager to greet every day, and very comfortable with my new grandmother status*. Through all their transitions, Tim and Sarah stayed in touch, despite living half a continent apart. How is their relationship today?

Sarah summarizes: *We are still very close and love each other very much. We get together at least once a year. Most recently, we went to meet our grandson and celebrate our son's graduation from grad school in Oregon. Tim's lover was there, as was my lover (aka husband!), so little Chris was cuddled by three of his four grandpas! Tim and I converse often on the phone and support one another in our concerns about aging parents, share our joy in our son and his family, and reminisce about our lives together.* Sarah's warmth is genuine. It is possible to move beyond the trauma and maintain even a loving friendship with a gay ex-mate.

Carol received a birthday card from Jim this past July. Written above his signature was this note: *Finally—an appropriate card that says what I feel! Hope your special day is wonderful. Love, Jim.* The printed message on the card said, *We've been friends forever—at least it seems like forever. We've been there for each other during some of life's most difficult times, sharing advice, wisdom, and comfort. We've been there for each other to applaud the daily victories and celebrate the life-changing events that only true friends could know the real importance of. We've been friends forever, and I hope that we never, ever stop, because you and your friendship mean the world to me.*

Carol was touched by the birthday message: *It has been more than a decade since Jim told me he's gay. I have experienced all the stages of grief and all the stages of straight spouse coping. This friendship is what we have left of our thirty-five-year marriage. It is good.*

SHIFTING SOCIAL AND FAMILY TIES

Besides discovering how to relate to a gay mate or ex-mate, straight spouses must also modify connections with all their other relationships—extended family on both sides, friends, and associates at work. In the throes of the early crisis of disclosure, you feel isolated from almost everybody. Often the veil of secrecy forces this isolation. Even after the secret is out, there are predictable shifts in relationships.

Maintaining a close tie to an ex-spouse's family is unusual and challenging. Even if closeness existed prior to the homosexual disclosure and subsequent separation, personal dynamics shift. A few people, like Lee, are able to retain the "family feeling" after divorce, but such an outcome seems rare. Now, several years later, she still enjoys seeing Randy's family. Her parents have not been so open about the divorce and overtly rejected Randy at first. Now, they have softened a bit, and Lee is relieved that lately they have begun to accept her continued friendship with her ex-husband.

Matt's outcome with Sharon's family is a more common scenario, related fully in Chapter 1. When Sharon came out, she promptly flew to Florida to tell her family. A letter from Matt that Sharon carried to her parents conveyed his understanding but also his great sadness. As their marriage dissolved, Matt hoped to remain close to Sharon's parents, since his own are deceased, but that has not happened. Sharon's family weaned away with time. They are cordial but have little contact with Matt. This is part of the loss he grieves. It's hard to hold on to the periphery when the center gives way.

Friendships also shift after any couple's separation, especially when one of the partners comes out. Jim and Carol were longtime friends with several other couples. They had traveled together, spent vacations together, and had run in the same social circles in Boulder for years. *I really thought that Jim's disclosure would not harm those friendships. But there were immediate changes. A subtle aloofness was noticeable. Many married couples are uncomfortable with a single friend, even one with a long history with the group. Perhaps they feel somehow threatened, either by the stigma of homosexuality in their midst, or by the very fact that one of their circle is newly single. My invitations from them slowed, then stopped.* Many of the straight spouses interviewed mentioned the same experience. It's probably natural and certainly predictable that couple friends drop away. There is simply less in common. Perhaps the best response for a straight spouse is to recognize their discomfort, accept it, and begin to form new friendships and deepen those with others who are single.

Younger people may adapt more quickly to shifting social and family ties. With less history, perhaps it is easier to let go of their past. Those in middle age (or older) may grieve their relationship losses more deeply and for a longer time. It may also be harder for them to reach out to new friends. Sooner or later, however, they pick themselves up and go back into the social stream. Carol took great solace in her women friends before she was brave enough to think about "dating" again. Lee gathered her courage and met new friends on the Internet. Sarah matched up with an old friend. When the two of them decided to marry, her gay ex attended her wedding with genuine joy. There are no rules for this rebuilding. It is a very personal and individual matter. The essential thing is somehow to find your own way out of isolation and to move on.

As this chapter demonstrates, when a gay mate comes out, the impact can be compared to dropping a pebble in still water. There is a splash at the center when the pebble hits the water, then circles of ripples move outward, one after the other, from their common center. The impact rocks the straight partner first, then the ripples move to the children and other close family, then to friends, and eventually to the workplace and outer world. As stages of coping are experienced (and sometimes repeated), the surface of the water finally calms. Sometimes, though, a straight partner continues to churn under the surface, challenged by long-term personal obstacles. These challenges are the subject of the next chapter.

QUESTIONS TO PONDER

1. What issues related to your mixed-orientation partnership trouble your family? Have your children reacted negatively? Are they accepting changes in the family dynamic? Take a step back and try to understand the overall effect of your partnership on close and extended family.
2. Assess your friendships and social life. Do you see gains or losses related to your changing relationship with your gay partner?
3. How do you feel about your gay mate now? Is friendship or closeness still possible?

ACTIVITY

Write in your journal a short description of your current relationship with your family, your gay partner, and your friends. Then write down what you would like those relationships to become. Imagine the very best outcome for all concerned and make an effort to bring it to fruition.

Chapter 8

Long-Term Personal Obstacles

The previous three chapters examined some common obstacles that surface shortly after a gay mate's disclosure. Almost every straight spouse experiences these immediate risks and their accompanying emotions, including fear and shame, anger and grief, and challenges related to children, extended family, and social ties. Working through such severe tests takes genuine courage.

Many straight spouses find the inner resources to move beyond their crisis without lasting psychological harm. Unfortunately, others struggle with long-term damage. Among these chronic problems are loss of trust, reluctance to commit to a new relationship, religious and moral conflicts, reiteration of a past wound, and resultant loneliness, depression, and bitterness. These deeper manifestations of hurt are obviously more difficult to heal, often taking months or years of therapy to conquer. This chapter will address some of the most common aftereffects.

LOSS OF TRUST

I am fearful that my negative experiences with my ex-spouse have and will prevent me from being open to a healthy relationship. Sandy's fear is well-founded. Inevitably, straight spouses suffer emotional wounds that manifest in loss of trust and frequently in a reluctance to commit to a new relationship. They desperately want intimacy but run for cover when someone new comes too close. They may have several transitional relationships while regaining their sense of self and their ability to trust others. During these brief interim associations, they may repeat familiar patterns they had with

When Your Spouse Comes Out
Published by The Haworth Press, Taylor & Francis Group, 2008. All rights reserved.
doi:10.1300/6046_08

the gay mate or, conversely, experiment with different relationship styles.

Seeing transitional connections as part of the healing process, without too much futuristic expectation, eases pressure to move too fast. Dating a person without thought of "forever" is preferable during the recovery of selfhood and trust. Instead, ask the realistic question, "Can the two of us benefit from spending time together?" It's beneficial to practice being single—a prerequisite for a healthy new partnership.

A candid conversation helped Sandy understand her own self-defeating pattern that had damaged several postdivorce relationships. *As a male friend of mine said, "I keep finding myself in relationships with strong women who have overcome one or many great obstacles, usually having to do with an ex-husband. What they don't seem to be able to do is stop fighting. I wish they wouldn't treat me as if I were guilty of his crimes. I'm innocent."*

To stop fighting is the task. Replete with memories and ingrained habits of response, straight mates repeat worn patterns. One enormous obstacle is the inner noise of old tapes that replay in their minds, tainting new relationships with negative messages. Unresolved internal struggles repeatedly haunt the present, like unhappy ghosts. A new friend or lover may unknowingly trip a trigger for earlier emotions—and pay the price. Carol's experience is typical: *Early in my second marriage, still recovering from my hurt, I often relapsed into unhealthy patterns, eliciting reminders (sometimes gentle, sometimes not) from my new husband: "I'm NOT Jim!" It took patience on his part and determined self-talk for me to stop my cycle of faulty assumptions and "cutting and running" when I felt afraid.*

Sandy's challenge is similar. She compares her previous life with her gay husband to Wendy with Peter Pan. *I was attracted to him because he was full of wild dreams and plans for adventures. What I learned over time was that being with a free spirit did not mean more freedom for me. What it meant for me was that I allowed myself to become more conservative, more of a killjoy, to provide some balance and grounding in our lives.* She sees her former husband as a boy who never grew up and her own role as his protector and defender. Her gentle side was compromised through repeated dramatic rescues. Anger often flared. She almost lost her feminine identity in those years, and her challenge now is to lighten up, to give voice again to her inner child and her gentle woman's spirit.

Since her divorce from James, Sandy has moved through several short-term relationships. Commitment is hard for her; complete trust still eludes her. She laments her loss wistfully: *I have tried to let go of the past and allow myself to be vulnerable enough to soften and be female. It still takes a conscious effort. I'm afraid!* "I'm afraid" sums it up. It appears that recovery of trust for a straight spouse is accomplished only after releasing the past, but it may take a long time to understand that love and hurt are not an equation.

To release the past, preliminary steps are required. We process the stages of grief and dampen anger. We begin to recover our sense of self-worth, allowing more openness to new relationships. We get comfortable being single. We drop the drama and stop the old mental tapes. Developing awareness and insight, we recognize unhealthy tendencies in time to do something different, to make a fresh start in a new situation.

The final important task is forgiveness. Without the baggage of resentment, we become free to love and trust again. Like so many others, Sandy recognizes her struggle with this step. *I'm not sure that I am fully recovered. I have not reached the point of forgiveness. If I get there, it will be a milestone in my family heritage. My family does not forgive easily, if ever. Instead they keep score, saving mental "Green Stamps" on people they feel have crossed them. As a friend once explained this process, it is fruitless, because you never get a full book. The analogy is even truer today, since I haven't even seen a Green Stamp book to hold them, or a store to redeem them, for more than twenty years.* If there are any stamp books on the shelf of your mind, they are a major source of inner conflict that prevents renewal of trust. It's time to throw them away. A quotation attributed to Confucius applies: "Those who cannot forgive others break the bridge over which they themselves must pass."

What can be done to facilitate renewal? Sandy is making steady progress and offers her strategy: *I feel that I am ready for a relationship, but it's not happening. I continue to divide the free time I cherish with friends, extended family, my daughter, and myself—having alone time. Obsessing about not being in a relationship won't change the situation, so I just focus on enjoying my time and letting life unfold.* It's good advice to live in the present moment, as Sandy describes, avoiding the tendency to rerun the past. This promotes openness to a happier future.

Writing in a journal also supports renewal. It's a tool that invites full expression of conflicted sides of the self. Let your inner critic vent. Pull the diatribe out. Write it; read it. Evaluate its validity. Then invite your compassionate nature to answer criticisms with loving-kindness. If additional inner voices growl for attention, give them expression in the journal as well. Is perfectionism or anger or grief a stumbling block? Be that trait and express its view. Let your inner child speak its sense of wonder—or cry out its pain. The simple act of writing down feelings helps release them and ease inner cacophony. The healing steps of awareness and insight grow through journaling.

Like the other long-term challenges discussed in this chapter, regaining trust takes time and patience. Professional counseling may assist recovery, and the rewards are worth the required risks and hard work. The payoff is to be happy—either as a single person or in a new partnership. Either way, you are a whole person, free of the burden of past heartbreak.

RELIGIOUS AND MORAL CONFLICTS

"The church, among other elements of society, has contributed to the persecution and suffering of homosexuals, and it is its culpability in this regard which provides one reason for seeking a more enlightened understanding." This 1977 affirmation by the General Assembly of the Christian Church, Disciples of Christ, urged the passage of legislation to "end the denial of civil rights and the violation of civil liberties for reason of sexual orientation." For decades, many mainstream religious organizations have made similar public statements supporting rights and liberties of all people. However, while they officially uphold equal treatment of gays, many individuals and congregations privately believe that homosexuality is a sin condemned by God. Prejudice against gays is therefore widespread, sometimes carried to the point of discrimination, subtle cruelty, and excommunication from some sects.

Moral conflict is inevitable for mixed-orientation couples that adhere to a condemning religion. Pressure builds from both ecclesiastical policy and from personal beliefs, making an already difficult situation almost unbearable. Greg and Donna's story is a poignant example. Their marriage of seventeen years appeared strong. Greg said, *I described our marriage to others at the time as near perfect. I had a neighbor come up to me just weeks before the divorce and say that she really wanted to have a marriage as good as mine.*

Greg and Donna had two children and were very active in their Latter-Day Saints (LDS; Mormon) church, where Donna and her friend, Lynn, worked with the teen group. Lynn was already divorced when she and her daughter became friends with Greg's family. They all got together often and especially enjoyed hiking and other outdoor activities.

But Donna seemed unhappy. She had suffered from mild depression for a long time. Greg was worried because they had no sexual intimacy and he didn't understand Donna's increasing emotional distance. Searching for some solution, they talked about making a fresh start in a new place. Soon, Greg accepted a new job in Colorado, to begin the coming January. Since it would be difficult for their teenage kids to transfer in the middle of a school year, it seemed best for Donna to stay behind, sell their Utah house, and finish the move when school ended in the spring. It wasn't a perfect solution but seemed to be the best plan.

Greg left for Colorado and Donna put their house on the market. He remembers the next six months as a lonely time: *During the time that I was in Colorado alone, Donna and the kids sold the house and moved in with Lynn until the end of the school year. When Donna visited me in Colorado, she would only come for very short periods of time. She made weak excuses to leave early to head back to Utah, and it was generally very stressful.*

When school ended in June, Donna and the youngsters completed the move to Colorado and joined Greg in their new home. Things got worse. *Donna's depression became very severe. She would take frequent trips back to Utah, didn't make much of an effort to make new friends, and was generally very unhappy. Whenever I suggested that she get counseling, she would reject the idea. One day in October, I finally kept at it until she said she knew counseling would do no good if she weren't willing to do anything about it. I had been wondering for quite some time, and had even asked a time or two, if she were lesbian. She always adamantly denied it. But this time, I told her that she needed to tell me what was going on, or our marriage was gone any-*

way. She finally admitted that she was lesbian and that she was in love with Lynn.

Like so many straight spouses, Greg had a moment of release. *My immediate reaction was one of relief. I figured that it really wasn't my problem all these years.* He also had a brief, predictable time of denial of the reality of the revelation. He asked, *Do you want to change? I told her that the only way I could keep trying with our marriage was if there was any way she could be heterosexual. She said that she had tried that for long enough to know that she couldn't but wanted to keep the marriage together for the kids. She wanted to stay married and fake it for another six years, until the kids were out of school, and then get divorced.*

Greg faced a familiar straight spouse dilemma. He was torn apart by his desire to protect his children and his own need to live a personally authentic life. For the next week Greg wrestled with the idea of hiding Donna's secret for six more years. *I hated to waste that much more of my life. I felt like I deserved a real marriage and thought that it was very hypocritical to carry on with a farce like that, just to end it as soon as the kids were out of school.* An agonizing week of uncertainty crawled past. *We finally decided to divorce, but not to tell the kids until they were out of school the next June.*

Donna continued to use their children as leverage to control Greg. Four more months passed and he became increasingly resentful about living the lie. Greg's lowest period was this time in the closet. He alternated feeling sorry for Donna and being angry and depressed. *I had a real feeling of having wasted seventeen years. I felt that I was bending over backward, protecting her interests and not taking care of myself.* His only confidant was his journal. He traveled with his work and wrote while sitting in airports, pouring his anxiety and pain onto page after page of his private book.

When he couldn't stand the secrecy any longer, Greg told his brother the truth. *Donna was very resistant to me telling anyone what was going on. She was furious with me when I did tell my family. She always put it in terms of protecting the kids, which I was very sensitive to. But it was really hard to go as long as I did without talking to others.*

Finally, they told their children the truth about their impending separation. Greg's greatest fear was *losing my kids over it. I was afraid that they wouldn't be able to handle it emotionally.* The family drove to Utah over the July 4th holiday. Once there, at Lynn's house, they first explained the situation to their sixteen-year-old boy. He was stunned and upset, then tried to protect his mother by aiming his hurt and anger toward Greg. Their fourteen-year-old daughter, on the other hand, was not surprised. She had noticed Donna's unusually loving interactions with Lynn for years and had guessed that her mother was lesbian. She wanted to stay in Colorado with Greg, but Donna enticed her back to Utah by using the church as a magnet: *Come home to your friends and your church.*

Greg was trapped by the family's religious convictions. The LDS doctrine holds that homosexuality is a sin, requiring excommunication from the church. If it is known that a person is gay, no participation in church activities is allowed. That was the power behind Donna's obdurate desire to keep her secret. If the truth came out, Lynn would lose her job and their Mormon congregation would ostracize them. Moreover, Greg couldn't tell his Utah friends the truth for fear of bringing judgment and shame on his daughter. Even more infuriating to him was that he bore all the blame. He was seen as the villain in the divorce. *I'm victimized by the lie that Donna lives. She's the poor, abandoned divorcée whose friend has taken her in. I'm even more concerned about my daughter, who has to carry her mother's secret every day.*

Another unfortunate fallout of the situation in Utah was that the daughter felt the need to prove her own heterosexuality and became somewhat promiscuous. Her brother, living with Greg in Colorado, simmered in anger. He acted out his rebellion through *really behaving poorly, doing badly in school, and smoking pot. He barely graduated from high school, then partied through his first semester of college.* Later, he lied about these forbidden activities—sex, alcohol, drugs—in order to pass the Mormon screening for mission work. Donna supported her son's dishonesty that allowed him to travel to Honduras as a missionary for the church. Greg felt angry and left out, while Donna was a full participant in the church—hiding behind her lies.

After the separation, Greg didn't know where to turn. *I didn't think I had any control of anything. I felt as though nothing was going right and there wasn't any hope of things changing.* Seeking counsel, Greg confided in his LDS bishop in Colorado, who responded that he would *blow the whistle and tell on Donna!* Devastated and disillusioned, Greg felt cheated of his heritage, though he still "feels Mormon" and is stressed by his root beliefs. His fear of losing his children was also well-founded. Ironically, they judge and resent their father because he has left the Mormon Church. Yet they do not judge their mother's dishonest lifestyle. It is a very confusing, multilayered conundrum.

Eventually, Greg was able to let go of his conflict and start over. He remarried, attends the Lutheran Church with his new family, and has reconciled with his daughter (but not completely with his son). He and Donna have become more cordial. *We do get along well enough to support the kids. We go to graduations and important events together and are able to discuss the kids' issues without conflict. Things aren't horrible, but there is an underlying tension whenever we're together.* Happier today, Greg says, *Divorce isn't the end of the world. I won't ever do it again, but one does survive.*

Greg's conflict about his lesbian wife was complicated greatly by their particular religion. Two irreconcilable forces that shaped their lives—religious beliefs and sexuality—impaled them both. While details differ, the pressure imposed by religious condemnation is widespread. It goes to the very core of one's being and leaves permanent emotional scars.

Fortunately, Greg is a survivor. Asked what advice he would give to a man whose wife is lesbian, he says, *Find people to talk to—especially find a _man_ who has gone through it to give that perspective.* Internet chat rooms also helped Greg. In retrospect, he can now cite some positive outcomes: *I think I am more resilient, more empathetic to others. I've learned to value myself more and to balance my needs with those of others.* Greg's struggle with the requirements of his church made his journey difficult, but certainly not unique. His story demonstrates the power that religious conviction holds in many private lives.

Throughout this book, personal stories of people like Greg and Sandy have illustrated discernible patterns and challenges straight spouses experience and pass through. In many cases, they make their passage without formal therapy. However, serious emotional pitfalls usually require professional help. In the remainder of this chapter, we examine some common, severe emotional states that recur, with signs for recognition and suggestions for alleviation. Depression, bitterness, loneliness, and the reiteration of a past wound are serious, long-term challenges. The analysis offered here is a starting point toward healing, but an underlying reality is the need for professional counseling to facilitate complete recovery.

DEPRESSION

The examples of Greg and Sandy in this chapter demonstrate how mixed-orientation marriage can create a complicated grieving process. Stress from secrecy, shame, betrayal, confusion, and isolation compounds the difficulty of completing the grief cycle and may lead to clinical depression. Mental health is in jeopardy during any shocking loss, particularly if there is a history of depression or a current struggle with it. Even well-adjusted and successful people may find themselves susceptible to overwhelming, debilitating symptoms. It's essential to recognize signs of depression to prevent a chronic condition, greater loss, and the risk of suicide.

While clinical depression has several distinct profiles, no two individuals experience this form of suffering in the same way. Self-help preventive steps for working through grief are listed in Chapter 6. However, identifiable warning signs indicate a pressing need for professional counseling or immediate intervention. In surveying the manifestations of depression discussed in the following paragraphs, you may be able to recognize yourself or a loved one in need of professional care.

Symptoms can be immediate and extremely intense, or less severe but spread over a longer period of time. Either condition, acute or chronic, can impair basic functioning and should be addressed fully. Emotional and cognitive signs of depression include a low mood, disinterest in life, inability to experience pleasure, feelings of worthlessness, excessive guilt, hopelessness, inability to think clearly, poor concentration, and suicidal thoughts or attempts (American Psychiatric Association, 1994). Physical symptoms may include insomnia, excessive sleeping, fatigue, poor appetite, eating or drinking too much, and extreme agitation. Anxiety, an extreme elevated state, or excessive activity may also mix or alternate with depression.

Warning signs vary in persistence and intensity. Certain indicators do determine whether a debilitating condition is chronic or severe. If you have noticed four or more of the symptoms listed here, you are at risk of depression. If you have experienced symptoms for more than six months, it is a chronic condition. Severe symptoms call for urgent action. Contact a friend, family member, or counselor to help determine immediate steps to seek relief.

If a depressed individual is not able to recognize the threat, others may need to directly intervene. Suicidal thoughts or plans are the most dangerous signals indicating urgent need for professional help. Consult a competent psychotherapist, professional counselor, clinical social worker, psychologist, or psychiatrist. All are trained to give meaningful support and respond to your immediate needs for safety.

Your choice of a therapist is important. To ensure the best possible outcome, find a professional who inspires your confidence. Ask people you trust for referrals. Search the local phone book or the Internet for suitable possibilities, then interview potential choices. Check credentials to ensure educational background, but don't ignore your instincts. This is a human relationship that should *feel* right, though intuition must be supported by evidence of the therapist's training and reliability.

It may be challenging to find an appropriate counselor in a rural area or small town. First, it is crucial to find someone who is not judgmental or shaming regarding homosexuality. Another obstacle may be the small number of counselors available. If you know most of the people in town through family, school, religious, social, or occupational contexts, it may be hard to engage an impartial therapist. Friendship also confuses the professional relationship. It may even be necessary to go to a nearby city for therapy.

Depression is a serious, long-term threat, so do whatever it takes to connect with an appropriate counselor. Your mental health is certainly worth a focused search for a therapist and a commute to a neighboring town.

BITTERNESS

Bitterness, the long-term outcome of hanging onto anger, is also the result of not completing the grief cycle. The person who suffers most is the one who harbors resentment or rage. When we understand the diverse expressions of anger as aspects of grief, we may find it easier to approach them with compassion and to treat ourselves with greater kindness.

For most of us, it is difficult to find the courage to see our own patterns of anger and resentment clearly. We get mixed messages about these challenging emotions. On one level, we may have internalized family or societal messages that "anger is bad" and should not be felt or expressed. On another level, we accept messages that injustice should be avenged harshly, and we become entrenched in the victim's role. Both denial and entrenchment can lead to dispiriting bitterness. Anger must be met and eventually resolved, even when it surfaces over several years in the grief process.

Bitterness is the solidification of an emotion that should have passed with time. It hardens our hearts and blocks future joy and happiness. We live in the past, centering on events that are not current reality. The maturation process involves learning to respect the seasons of the grief cycle, the ebb and flow of emotions, and the intricacies of individual response to loss. It takes time—but not forever. Resigning yourself to a miserable life because you feel wronged or victimized is eating the rat poison in Pema Chödrön's example. The rat will not die because you have swallowed the toxin of resentment or martyrdom. Only *you* suffer its noxious, long-term effects.

Your identity as the unknowing spouse of a gay person, a role that you did not choose, is meant to pass. Everyone is on a different timetable, but working through the grief and anger may take a minimum of two years in the least complicated situation. The loss of a mate is one of life's hardest passages, and the longer the marriage, the more prolonged the grief. This and other complex factors may extend your personal process. If grief has been delayed or inhibited, you may deal with the emotions of sadness or anger for several years beyond your initial loss.

Assistance in the recovery process comes from various sources. Feedback from friends and family may be reliable or totally off the mark. Finding someone who listens well and understands the grief cycle is most useful. This can be a professional or a person who has experienced this crisis, survived it, and learned to thrive in spite of it. Paying attention to your own thoughts is also invaluable. Trustworthy clues are often discovered in your journal, recording your thoughts and reactions on the spot.

The companionship you choose on this journey of healing is crucial. Notice whether your confidant(e) fans the flame of anger or is genuinely interested in listening and understanding. People who feed anger or suggest that you leapfrog over this stage of grief often carry their own baggage of bitterness or unresolved pain. Nothing solidifies bitterness more than reinforcement from well-meaning cohorts who are stuck in anger themselves. Avoid them.

Instead, decide to heal. Set your intention to be free from your barrier of bitterness. This work begins with awareness and compassion for yourself. Old emotional walls were built to protect and defend from further pain and disappointment. Construction materials included all the forms of boundary disturbances that blocked genuine contact from others. These blocks, fully discussed in Chapter 4, include introjection, confluence, retroflection, projection, and deflection. Review the exercises in that chapter to gain further insight, then take appropriate action to tear down archaic walls that block the full and loving life you deserve.

LONELINESS

Humans have a remarkable capacity for contented aloneness when they feel secure and accept themselves and others. Without a ground of genuine relatedness, however, people are afraid to be alone and have a minimal tolerance for separation. Loneliness is a habitual state of disconnection from others and from the rich interior experience of our own wholeness.

A mate's coming out precipitates tremendous feelings of loneliness in the straight partner. Feelings are confused and it may be impossible to label or distinguish separate emotions from a general sense of unhappiness. Separation and divorce practically guarantee an extended pattern of loneliness. As time passes, unresolved grief isolates us further, marked by phantom relationships from our past and fear-based fantasies of the future. As loneliness increases, it further debilitates a depressed and bitter victim.

The habits of a lonely person are often expressed in unconscious behaviors and attitudes that reinforce one another. We are typically blind to the invisible walls we create in the ways we talk to ourselves or interact with others. Unless these isolating barriers are recognized and removed, the same patterns of loneliness are repeated in the next relationship or as a single person. Heartbroken straight spouses often isolate in this way. Individuals unwittingly spin a lonely cocoon through a series of small decisions that avoid intimacy and long-term commitment. Following the action steps to mitigate boundary distur-bances is a way to begin unraveling this cocoon, dispelling unre-solved grief and fear. Consider the exercises in Chapters 4 and 5 for some effective ways to reverse isolating behaviors.

We are vulnerable creatures. Life offers no guarantee of happiness, except by developing our own peace of mind. Although loss is inevi-table, renewal is possible. Our grief process is like a winter storm when we shutter the windows to protect a fragile heart from the cold blasts of the outer world. Our basic loving nature seeks warmth at the hearth of trust. Talking with others who have weathered the outer storm is like sitting by a tempered fire, melting the ice of bitterness and loneliness. In this comforting place, we can nurture acceptance and compassion necessary for healing.

Recovering from long-term loneliness begins with small steps to-ward awareness, insight, and action. Become intimate friends with the voices that make up the composite of your whole self. Cultivate curiosity, gentleness, and warmth toward the varied expressions of your inner being, learning to accept your own thoughts, feelings, and sensations. This deep knowing takes time. Often we don't want to hear the voice of the whiny brat, the wounded child, or the one with sexual hunger. Interior listening and acceptance are acquired skills that break the pattern of inner separation. Help is usually required to develop these skills. If you are unable to identify anyone in your im-mediate circle you can trust with this private process, a counselor or psychotherapist can be your guide.

Nurturing unconditional friendliness toward yourself, you can take the next steps into the outer world. Venture into deeper contact with all types of beings, from a mossy rock, to the clerk at the grocery store, to a new friend. Practice contact every day. Open your eyes. Start small and get in touch with the arts, nature, spiritual practice, sports, and pets. Notice how outdated defense mechanisms interfere with genuine contact with other people and the natural world. Enjoy the positive effects of changing these ingrained patterns and loneli-ness begins to dissolve. The discovery of a future long-term compan-ion or loved one starts with everyday interactions that gradually open a closed heart to love. Relish the adventure!

REITERATION OF A PAST WOUND

A major life crisis stresses our psychological state much as a raging storm strains a ship at sea. Unhealed experience from the past is like a leaky patch over a hole in the hull. If earlier emotional wounds have not completely healed, regression to habitual developmental patterns of managing distress rips the patch away and may sink the ship completely.

The full impact of a previous trauma often doesn't register until loss strikes later in life. Many problems are met with ineffective coping strategies that seem to work until a new crisis hits. What was buried in the forgotten past or occurred when we were too young to remember surfaces in troubling somatic symptoms, projections onto others, or personal reactions based in fear. Depression, bitterness, and loneliness are likely to be compounded when we do not pay close attention to these warning signs. That's the danger of an emotional crisis.

However, crisis also presents an opportunity—a chance to heal emotional wounds that have been blocking happiness all along. The Chinese symbol for "crisis" is made up of two picture signs, one for danger and the other for opportunity. Terrible misfortune may transform into opportunity, the impetus to grow stronger psychologically and eventually to live a fully satisfying life.

It is important to keep both danger and opportunity in mind. At the height of crisis, personal survival can trump meeting our higher needs for belonging, esteem, and actualization (Maslow, 1968). Simply fulfilling basic needs for proper nutrition, health, and safety at home can require enormous energy. If any of these fundamental needs were unmet during childhood, current survival may feel impossible. You feel threatened at a core level if your childhood sense of belonging suffered damage and was not fully restored. If self-worth or self-esteem were wounded and not healed, you may feel devoid of personal value. If self-actualization has escaped you, dreams and freedom may seem utterly impossible to achieve. Conscious awareness of considerable or extreme difficulty with any of these particular stages, from physical safety, to belonging, to self-esteem and self-actualization, will assist the healing process.

Each stage of developmental need builds on the one before, and learning to meet each is necessary to manifest our highest capacity.

But no one masters every stage perfectly, and personal disaster will reveal a weakness at any previous stage. You must seek assistance. At the height of despair, drop bravado, rise above embarrassment or shame, and call for help. Crisis should not be faced alone.

Earlier defenses that worked in childhood fall apart in an adult disaster. In fact, immature approaches make the situation worse. Rather than forcing your way through the chaos with old tools or collapsing in helplessness, seize the opportunity to grow beyond childhood survival strategies. Psychotherapy and counseling offer necessary support to survive your ordeal. Get help to heal the wounds of the past and simultaneously learn new skills to attain your future dreams.

QUESTIONS TO PONDER

1. Do I recognize myself in any of these long-term challenges: loss of trust, reluctance to commit, religious or moral conflict?
2. Do I presently suffer from depression, bitterness, or loneliness?
3. Am I repeating old patterns that reiterate a past wound, or that perpetuate it?

ACTIVITIES

1. Review the questions and self-help activities in Chapter 4. Using those exercises, work with your remaining issues.
2. Write in your journal any current challenges.
3. If you feel overwhelmed and unable to cope with these or other personal challenges, engage a counselor or therapist.

Part III: Fruition— Thriving After Crisis

Chapter 9

Secrets of Transformation

When a mate comes out, everyone involved treks a foreign trail. A straight spouse's journey is fraught with emotional peril and daunting challenges, but each conquered obstacle adds strength and wisdom. Many learn to see this life episode as just that—one event among many in a varied, extraordinary history. Though disorienting, the experience of a mixed-orientation relationship can actually become a gateway to unexpected opportunities for personal growth. It isn't the end of the world; it can be the beginning of something even better.

This final chapter points out some of the co-emergent wisdom realized by the men and women who populate this book. Their case studies in previous chapters held clues about how they freed themselves from the past and redirected their lives. Their discoveries are summarized at the end of this chapter. But first, one topic remains to be explored more deeply: Finding purpose that nourishes the spirit. For many, an ongoing inner hunger, woven throughout their experience, emerged with new importance.

When Your Spouse Comes Out
Published by The Haworth Press, Taylor & Francis Group, 2008. All rights reserved.
doi:10.1300/6046_09

LIVING "ON PURPOSE"

"Find out who you are, and do it on purpose." Country singer Dolly Parton's assertion touches deep truth. Finding a path that invigorates mind and spirit appears essential for complete straight spouse recovery. To live "on purpose" implies finding some meaningful cause, work, activity, philosophy, or value system that engages and uplifts. It feeds the need to give back. It nourishes the soul. This captivating purpose is very individual and was expressed in various ways in the interviews. Mark thrives on adventure, calling himself a *devout follower of the gods of serendipity.* For Bonnie, it's the church; for Zhi, it's caring for animals at the humane society; for Claire, it's calligraphy practice; for Lydia, it's teaching elders to write their memoirs. Some write books, others teach or garden or meditate or pray. Many find a religious or spiritual direction that fulfills them. Others return to school to develop latent talent or launch a new career in keeping with their sense of purpose.

One such straight spouse is Helen. Helen presently has a very healthy perspective about her first marriage to a gay man. When her husband of seven years told her that he was in love with a man, she felt the usual shock and relief but also felt excited. *Something interesting was actually happening. We both hoped he was bisexual. He wasn't.*

She experienced all the common stages of coping during the year that they stayed together in the closet. She blamed herself at first, then went through depression and a self-destructive period. *It took me a long time to recognize the anger I felt toward my family and the culture that taught me that if I was "good" I would live happily ever after. Then I was angry at myself for believing them.* These emotional states are familiar to most straight spouses. But Helen eventually got through it all, entered graduate school to finish an advanced degree, and remarried. *It took the time it needed.*

Today, rather than dwelling on the pain of her first marriage, she understands its positive outcome. *I see his homosexuality as a liberating force in my life. I was freed from following cultural and family scripts. I discovered myself and my own longings and gifts. I was liberated to find a soul mate in my present husband of fifteen years.* Describing her current feelings about her gay ex-husband, she says, *I like him, but I'm very glad we're not married. We are good friends—*

celebrate each other's birthdays. I know his partner of twenty-one years. He knows my husband and stepsons.

Helen attributes a good part of her recovery to her spiritual renewal. *I rediscovered my faith in God, returned to graduate work in theology, and am ordained to the ministry. This would not have been my path before. My husband's homosexuality freed me. I could never have been this happy with him, even if he had been straight.*

An author as well as a minister, Helen has published four books on spirituality and prayer. Looking back, she relates her most valuable lessons: *God loves me; I am loved; I am free to choose; I can survive. At sixty-two, I couldn't be happier. I feel I have entered my most creative decade.* Helen's "liberation" recalls a similar nugget from another world wisdom tradition, the sayings of the Buddha: "At the end of the journey, freedom. Until then, patience."

TOOLS FOR RENEWAL

There are no esoteric "secrets" for total recovery. It is simpler and yet more complicated than that, requiring a focused effort to change your mind. John Milton wrote, "The mind is its own place, and in itself can make a heaven of hell, a hell of heaven" (*Paradise Lost,* I, 254-255). Bonnie, from the case study in Chapter 1, takes the idea even further: *Go through the necessary steps of grieving your loss, then pick up the pieces, call upon your spirituality, and move on with your life, knowing that others have survived and that time heals. We have choices, and we can choose how long we want to be angry or sad (two days, two weeks, twenty-two years?). With God's help, with family, and with friends, we can choose to have a healthy, happy, meaningful life.* Bonnie's present fulfillment proves the truth of her words.

While there is no guaranteed fix, certain suggestions did surface repeatedly in the interviews for this book and in related literature. As Bonnie indicated, evidence of personal power emanates from most of the scarred but recovered straight mates on these pages. Along with this power is the responsibility to heal ourselves through choice and effort. How can this be done? The tools are at hand. Here are some of the most effective:

1. Take care of your health with plenty of exercise and a nutritious diet. A strong body is necessary to supply the energy needed for full emotional recovery.
2. "Relax as it is." Change the aspects of your situation that you have control over, but accept the things you cannot improve.
3. Keep talking. Use your confidant(e) or counselor as a safety valve for emotion. Feel your feelings and talk about them with a close friend or relative. Continue to write in your journal.
4. Get a pet. Having a living being to love and care for is therapeutic.
5. Use all available outside resources. Study this book and others that promote recovery. Search the Internet for information and support. Join a Straight Spouse Network chapter or use the Web site (www.straightspouse.org) to contact others who understand your experience.
6. Cultivate curiosity about the larger world. Develop new, constructive interests and activities that move you outside your personal problems. Take a class, start a new hobby, learn a new skill, or take a vacation to a place you've never seen.
7. When confidence allows, reach out to new friends who have a positive outlook. Avoid people who carry and reinforce anger and resentment.

These actions lead to excellent results for many straight spouses. The suggestions were repeated so often in the interviews, they approach a formula for recovery.

NOURISHING THE SPIRIT

Perhaps the most important step is hardest to define because it is so individual. That is nourishment of the spirit. Both research and personal experience strongly indicate that the ability to let go of resentment and forgive is paramount for ultimate recovery. As the speaker/philosopher Wayne Dyer points out, it isn't the snakebite that kills you, it's the venom. Until we let go of negativity, we cannot be whole. This idea is not new! The Chinese philosopher Confucius taught it 2,500 years ago: "Those who cannot forgive others break the bridge over which they themselves must pass." How can we begin this essential task of forgiveness?

An underlying difficulty is confusing the individual with the act. We can reject the actions that hurt us without hating the actor. This subtle differentiation allows more charity toward that person. Try to put yourself in the other person's place to understand that he or she has pain, just as you do. We can also call on our higher power, whatever form that takes, to help us let go of resentment.

If we have hurt another person ourselves, we can try to make amends, fix whatever we can, and then forgive ourselves as well. Sometimes we can't mend the ties with the person we wounded. In that case, we can use our good intentions to help someone else. Service to others is a proven method of self-healing.

It is also extremely important to stay in the present moment. Notice any tendency to replay your story line and relive your past dramas. Stop those old tapes and make a fresh start. Take a deep breath and be here now! Developing your spiritual side helps this process tremendously, building a foundation for positive intention and aspiration.

Finally, open your heart to new purpose in your renewed life. Set fresh goals to pursue with energy. You have much to give. One concrete way to support your path is to affirm your own worth. Give yourself positive encouragement with self-talk that builds your confidence. Repeat affirmations that are meaningful to you. Here are some examples: "I am a whole and worthwhile person, with or without a partner. I have everything I need to lead the life I choose. I can do this!" Practice staying in the present with these sayings or others you devise. These methods really work.

Activities for Nourishing the Spirit

1. Let go of resentment.
2. Forgive.
3. Make amends to others for harm you've done, and then forgive yourself as well.
4. Accept what can't be changed; recognize the limits of your control over past situations.
5. Stay present in the present!

HEALING FROM WITHIN

A straight mate's progression to wholeness is similar to the healing of a physical wound. It is an appropriate metaphor.

- Shock follows the crisis of breaking a bone.
- Surviving is the urgent need. The break is assessed and a splint and first aid are administered.
- The bone is carefully set in the right direction and supported by a cast for proper healing.
- Healing slowly takes place, encouraged by healthful choices and good medicine. The bone begins to mend from the inside.
- Growth and vigor become apparent, as the broken place builds new layers of protective strength, also created from within.
- Restoration and vitality result, as the healed bone is stronger than before, reinforced by the restorative process.

Like the bone in the metaphor, a wounded spouse can survive the break, pass through the crisis, set a good direction, heal from within, and grow stronger and more vital as a result of the experience. Others have done this. You can too.

After its initial pain, the experience of a mixed-orientation relationship can be a doorway, not a disaster. We have learned from the case studies that releasing resentment is the turning point toward full recovery. Healing then progresses through forgiveness, releasing the past, acceptance, and renewal of trust. The stories of Phil, Bonnie, Lee, Sarah, Mark, and Helen are just a few of the examples cited in this book. These are successful straight spouse "graduates" who re-created whole lives with purpose, worthy goals, and freedom from regret. In sharing their wisdom, they encourage and motivate others to help themselves in similar ways. They prove that it is possible.

Appendix A

Activities for Self-Healing

This appendix is a compilation of all the "Questions to Ponder" and "Activities" that appear throughout the book. They are reprinted here for easy reference and review, particularly for use by support groups, classroom instructors, and therapists working with straight spouses. Ultimately, though, straight mates are responsible for their own recovery and can effectively work independently with these tools. These exercises focus attention on the psychological forces at work and assist motivated people on their individual healing paths.

PART I: GROUND—
UNDERSTANDING CONTRASTING PATTERNS

Chapter 1: Three Straight Spouse Stories

Preparation for This Course in Recovery

After each chapter of this book, you are asked to ponder key questions and write your impressions, feelings, and responses in a journal. This is a critical element in your healing. It is a dialogue between you and the real people on the pages of this textbook for recovery. Keeping a journal is a very private activity, not an academic exercise. It is meant for your personal use, to be shared only when you choose, or not at all. Therefore, it should contain only absolutely authentic, totally honest answers to the questions posed, expanded by any other ideas or thoughts that come to you at the time. Your journal belongs only to you, so you can turn off that inner critic and just write. It is a record of your growth and evolution into wholeness. Later, you may look back and be proud of healthy progress.

When Your Spouse Comes Out
Published by The Haworth Press, Taylor & Francis Group, 2008. All rights reserved.
doi:10.1300/6046_10

Questions to Ponder

1. Is your pattern as a straight spouse similar to Kim's or Matt's or Bonnie's?
2. If you recognize yourself in one of these histories, is there something you'd like to change about your own response?
3. What clues can you discern in these three stories for more constructive action?

Activity

Purchase a new spiral-bound notebook for your journal. Use it only for this purpose, and write in it after reading each chapter—or as often as you feel the urge to express your thoughts. "Questions to Ponder" will get you started. Write your own story as you progress through this book. Start with your answers to the previous questions: How are you like the people you've just read about? How is your situation different? Your journal can offer insights and eventually guidance on your unique path of healing. Write honestly and spontaneously for your most important audience: YOU.

Chapter 2: Coming Out Three Ways

Questions to Ponder

Given your own mixed-orientation dilemma, try to picture yourself in the happiest, healthiest situation possible. Dream a little! Imagine your ideal outcome in vivid detail. Envision yourself in that best-case scene. Can you think of a first step toward that dream?

Activities

1. Write in your journal a description of your imagined ideal outcome. Try to "see" it and feel it in living color and exquisite detail.
2. Check the local availability of a straight spouse support group. Look for PFLAG in the phone book and check the PFLAG and SSN (Straight Spouse Network) Web sites for more resources and information: www.pflag.org and www.straightspouse.org. Visit a support group meeting, if possible.

Chapter 3: Steps Toward Resolution

Questions to Ponder

Review the stages of coping at the beginning of this chapter.

1. Can you identify where you stand today in that process?
2. Have you experienced any, or all, of these stages?
3. Have you repeated any of the stages?
4. Does it help to know that millions of others have felt as you do?

Activity

After writing your thoughts on these questions in your journal, identify a trusted person to confide in. Share your experience regularly with a relative or friend, or ask for a phone contact of another straight spouse from SSN or PFLAG. Consider group or individual therapy. Talking to an understanding, supportive confidant(e) may help clarify your options.

PART II: PATH—
SELF-HEALING GUIDE FOR STRAIGHT SPOUSES

Chapter 4: Underlying Psychological Forces

Questions to Ponder on Introjection

1. What societal introject (internal message) have I assumed without questioning? Does it fit for me? Do I choose to keep it, alter it, or re- ject it?
2. What family messages were positive? What family messages were negative? Is there an old tape that makes it difficult to like myself or make choices for myself?
3. What positive message would I choose for myself at this time of diffi- culty?

Activities Related to Introjection

1. Write down several believed thoughts that are presently getting in your way. Try to identify their original source. For a period of one to four weeks make a commitment to notice how one of these repeated ideas enters your thinking or behavior throughout the day. Be gentle with yourself! When you become aware of an introject, appreciate

your new awareness and replace it with a positive message to your-self. Note in your journal when you were able to practice this aware-ness exercise and how you felt. This is a challenging practice; con-gratulate yourself even for small progress.
2. Continue this practice with other internalized messages you have identified. This exercise can be particularly helpful after a difficult en-counter with your spouse, friend, or family member that may trigger shame or self-blame.

Questions to Ponder on Confluence

1. Is it difficult to know what I truly want?
2. Do I have a hard time making decisions when others are involved?
3. Do I let others choose for me?
4. Do I notice myself, family members, or my spouse using the word "we" to express an individual opinion, choice, or desire?

Activities Related to Confluence

1. If this is a boundary disturbance you struggle with, commit to bring conscious awareness to confluent speech and behaviors in yourself and others. Replace the word "we" with "I" and notice how it feels. Be patient with yourself and others in the process. Every time you detect the pattern, appreciate your new awareness and write in your journal about your feelings and experiences.
2. Notice how you feel when others use the royal "we." Remember that the word received royal connotation because kings and queens as-sumed the court was always aligned with their sentiments and needs! Nevertheless, in this exercise it is not your job to correct others. In-stead, be wary of messages that blur your boundaries and confuse your relationships. You can learn to see the habit clearly and decide instead to define yourself independently, even in the face of resis-tance.
3. Each day select an activity that is specifically tailored to your own needs and desires. Start small. Record the activities and your progress in your journal.

Questions to Ponder on Retroflection

1. Do I have physical mannerisms or symptoms that may be rooted in retroflection?
2. Am I prone to accidents, illness, or injuries at this time? Are chronic physical problems worse than usual?

3. Do I seldom or never feel the emotion of anger in my body?
4. Do I say negative things to myself when something goes wrong in my environment or with other people?
5. Do I judge myself harshly for being in a relationship with someone who is gay?

Activities Related to Retroflection

1. If you answer yes to any of these questions, make a commitment to address one of your retroflective behaviors in the next one to four weeks. Begin by cultivating daily awareness of its presence in your thoughts or body. Remember that this new awareness is not another opportunity to beat yourself up! Instead, appreciate your progress. If the retroflection is a tension, pain, or habit in your body, focus your attention into the area, slow your breathing, and relax for a moment. If the pattern occurs in your thoughts, notice what you say to yourself and let it go. Then replace your self-inflicted negativity with something kind and positive.
2. Write about your experiences with these exercises in your journal, noting any small changes in thoughts and actions. Deep-seated patterns will take time to reverse, but recognize that any new awareness indicates beneficial progress.

Questions to Ponder on Projection

1. Am I in a relationship where the expression of feelings is distributed in a lopsided manner? Is this a family pattern for me or for my spouse?
2. Is there one particular emotion, such as anger or grief, that I do not express? Is there an emotion that I continually feel and/or express? Am I unable to feel anything? Are any of these patterns of behavior in evidence in other family members, now or in my childhood? What about my partner's family?
3. How is the difficult behavior of my spouse like one of my parents or siblings? What unfinished business with this family member intensifies my painful emotional response to my mate?

Activities Related to Projection

1. When issues from the family of origin compound a current relationship crisis, the challenge can be daunting and overwhelming. First, understand that most marital and family difficulties are entangled with our cultural, personal, and childhood histories. This basic understanding helps us see beyond self-blame and recrimination. Next, commit to identifying one pattern of behavior that has its roots in the process of

projection. Notice what emotion is most tied to this behavior. Also note your self-talk about your actions and feelings. Write your observations in your journal and share your insights with a close friend or counselor.

2. Practice identifying a pattern of projection in your daily actions for one to four weeks. Each time, remind yourself that your response is influenced or intensified by past experience. Slowly <u>breathe</u> to help relax in the moment. After practicing this exercise for a while you will begin to notice that your emotional response lessens over time.

NOTE: This exercise is not suggested if you have serious abuse or neglect in your family history, as it may compound or intensify your emotional response. If you discover this occurring, you should seek professional help.

Questions to Ponder on Deflection

1. Do I use deflection to avoid staying with emotions, bodily sensations, or intuitions? How do I do this?
2. Do I use deflection to avoid contact with others? How do I do this?
3. What avoidance behaviors do I observe in my partner and others in my immediate circle at this time? How do their actions affect how I feel and respond?

Activities Related to Deflection

1. Choose one deflective behavior (avoidance pattern) you have identified in yourself that you would like to change. Commit to gently bring attention to moments when you automatically engage in this habit. At first you may feel dismayed or judge yourself for how often you notice your pattern. Conscious attention to this defense mechanism will eventually decrease its frequency.

After a couple of weeks you may add a means of contact that your behavior was cutting short. For example, if you avoid eye contact, make an effort to look more directly when talking with someone else. If you notice a tendency to change the subject when the conversation feels personal, allow yourself to stay a little longer with your feelings and the topic at hand.

It's a good idea to begin this exercise when your emotions are not highly charged and with individuals who do not feel threatening. Remember that small changes can make a big difference. Increased contact can bring you closer to people who could help you at this time. Your journal can also be a good friend when you write down your feelings and observations on a regular basis.

2. When you notice how others habitually deflect their attention, concentrate awareness on your own feelings and reactions to their behavior. Dispassionate observance opens more options for response. For example, if your partner often changes the subject, you can bring the conversation back to the central topic. It is better to assert your own interests, rather than trying to change someone else by labeling him or her "wrong."

This exercise is useful with friends and family who want to be supportive yet have deflective patterns that obstruct healing. Such people may avoid contact, change the subject, or suggest that you not cry. Identify at least one person as a close contact when you need to share feelings. Say that you need to cry or talk and just have someone listen for a short time. If there is no one in your circle who is capable of learning this skill, it is important to find a counselor or therapist, so you don't feel completely alone.

Chapter 5: Immediate Personal Challenges

Fear

1. Awareness of Fear
   - Watch for fight behaviors:
     —Feelings of rage and anger
     —Arguments
     —Hurting yourself (retroflections)
   - Watch for flight behaviors:
     —Compulsive busyness or overwork
     —Denial (saying things like, "It's not that bad," or "My partner will change")
     —Distractions (watching too much TV, caretaking others instead of yourself)
   - Watch for freeze behaviors:
     —Holding your breath
     —Numbed feelings
     —Isolating and keeping secrets
     —Inability to get out of bed, off the couch, or out of the house
2. Insight into Fear
   - Watch how your thoughts connect to bodily sensations.
   - Learn from self-observation your primary reactive defense patterns.
   - Use knowledge of your fear patterns for self-understanding, not self-rebuke.
   - Realize your present situation is not the future.

- Talk with others experienced in the loss and personal crisis of gay–straight relationships.
3. Action Steps to Counter Fear
   - Actively and systematically witness sensations, thoughts, and behaviors. Commit to check in with your internal process three times throughout the day and write your observations in a daily journal.
   - Remember to slow down and breathe when you're aware of a fear response.
   - Without judgment, label thoughts "past" or "future," then come back to the present moment by bringing your attention to slowing your breath.
   - Without judgment, notice if thoughts of the past are fueling anger or hopelessness, or if they are helping you move forward. It can be useful to set aside a special time of day to review and grieve. This can assist you in containing the largest feelings to keep them from erupting when you are on the job, with your children, or during other activities.
   - Again, without judgment, notice if thoughts about the future hold negative images, or if you are problem solving and envisioning better possibilities.
   - Immediately replace negative mental images with a calming image. Create a simple mental picture that represents peace to you. It can be anything that's personally comforting, perhaps a favorite mountain lake, a calm ocean, or a gentle butterfly. Consistently use this mental picture to replace one that is disturbing or painful.
   - When you notice negative self-talk, immediately repeat a phrase that reminds you of a centered, peaceful state. It could be wisdom borrowed from a poem or religious tradition or a simple sentence like, "Peace is in my heart." Use the same phrase repeatedly to replace self-criticism and inward scorn.

Shame

1. Awareness of Shame
   - Identify shame-based introjects in negative self-talk and behaviors.
   - Identify past and current sources of shaming. Notice the specific actions of others that trigger shame feelings. Does this remind you of someone in your past?
   - Track your self-esteem several times each day for a week. Confident? Doubting? Insecure? Low opinion of self? Self-loathing? Objectivity grows as you note fluctuations in your sense of self, and close observation demonstrates that feelings are not permanent.

- Identify words or actions of your friends, family, and spouse that arouse shame.
- Learn to recognize shame based on homophobic societal messages you receive in association with your mate.
- Regularly note in your journal your awareness of these categories of shame. Getting it out of your system and onto paper is healing in itself.

2. Insight into Shame
   - Observe whether you rigidly categorize thoughts and actions into good or bad. Gently replace this labeling with observation and curiosity toward the source of these judgments.
   - Note the difference between your old mental tapes (introjects) and your own present values. Make a list of your values and which thoughts and actions support these principles. Note what undermines them.
   - Replace labeling thoughts and actions as "good" and "bad" with "helpful" and "unhelpful."
   - Distinguish between rules or standards you have been given and which ones make sense at this time in your life. Notice when you are a perfectionist or a rebel against the rules. Decide what is "good enough" by your own standards.

3. Action Steps to Counter Shame
   - Talk through feelings of shame with a psychotherapist.
   - Allow yourself time to make important decisions. Do not make decisions based on shame. Recognize the possibility of changing your mind.
   - Maintain self-care habits throughout crisis periods and when you feel low. Resist the tendency to drop healthful activities when under stress.
   - Practice the four-step process to communicate your fundamental needs and make requests. Read *Nonviolent Communication* by Marshall Rosenberg (2005) to increase your effectiveness and confidence.
   - Increase activities that reduce stress and promote relaxation. Take more walks, hot baths, and time alone or with friends and pets. Listen to music, read, bake, garden, or do whatever you enjoy that does not impose outside pressure.
   - Make regular appointments for massage and other health tune-ups.
   - Appreciate yourself for recognizing shame-based introjects. Create a brief positive statement to replace a core negative message you have identified (such as, "I value myself," "I am worthy of respect," "I belong"). Repeat it immediately whenever you experience shame.

Chapter 6: Lingering Risks, Anger, and Grief

Anger

1. Awareness of Anger
   - Observe the physical sensations that arise when you feel angry. Then focus internally, slow your breath by inhaling and exhaling fully, and notice any changes in your awareness.
   - Pay attention to the physical sensations of retroflection. Focus, slow your breath, and note any shifts in your awareness.
   - Examine any judgments you have toward sensations of anger, such as "I shouldn't feel this way." What changes when you let go of this thought, slow your breath, and focus on the physical sensations? Each time anger arises, repeat this simple exercise and see how the emotion dissipates over time with awareness and kindness toward your self.
2. Insight into Anger
   - Replace judgment with curiosity. Ask yourself, "Have I ever felt this angry before? When? What in my past makes anger so scary? What tools do I have to work with anger? How do I choose to work with anger now?"
   - Observe when anger alerts you to injustice, abuse, or mistreatment. Use your awareness to address situations that need to be corrected.
   - Observe how anger is a label we attach to a combination of thoughts and bodily sensations. When else do you feel this much energy in your system? Imagine turning this energy into something positive for yourself or others.
3. Action Steps to Work with Anger
   - Engage in regular physical exercise (not overdoing it at the height of rage).
   - Find a location where you can vent anger by beating a pillow or yelling. Do not hurt yourself. You may discover grief beneath your rage when you fully express yourself.
   - Express your rage with someone in a letter you will never send. This may release feelings you can't directly express to the person. You will also be more capable of expressing your concerns rationally after verbally or physically venting privately.
   - Confide in someone who can accept your anger without judgment and without provoking you to destructive actions.

Grief

1. Awareness of Grief
   - Recognize the stages of grief:
     —Denial
     —Anger

   —Bargaining
   —Depression
   —Acceptance
 • Develop an inner witness to these stages through continued obser-
   vation and identification of the signs of each stage. Notice the order
   of the stages in your experience. Which stage is most difficult or
   persistent? Which do you try to avoid?
2. Insight into Grief
 • Observe if your grief is complicated by factors other than a mixed-
   orientation marriage:
   —Circumstances out of the normal range of experience
   —Multiple losses
   —Trauma
   —Isolation
   —Polarized feelings toward the loved one (often due to a painful
     history together)
 • Develop your insight into a compassionate view. Note whether
   your analysis of the stages of grief reflects a cynical or defeatist at-
   titude. Reverse this process by reviewing the material and return-
   ing to the awareness phase.
 • Reflect on grief as a natural process. Remember that all change in-
   volves loss and requires a degree of letting go before life can begin
   anew.
3. Actions to Complete Grief
 • Recognize any denial and commit to living one day at a time.
 • Take time to process anger and resentment, as directed previously
   in this chapter.
 • Stop bargaining by looking for real solutions. Seek guidance in inspirational books, lectures, and shared stories of recovery.
 • Give yourself time, space, and companionship through periods of
   depression. Allow emotional, verbal, and physical expression of
   grief.
 • Commemorate your acceptance of loss and release the past through
   a ritual, activity, or ceremony. Private or shared events can help
   mark the beginning of a new life. You might consider a journey,
   spiritual retreat, gathering of the people who have supported you,
   or an expression in poetry, art, music, or dance.

Questions to Ponder

 1. What am I most afraid of right now?
 2. What am I most angry about?
 3. What is my greatest loss?
 4. What threatens me most about this?
 5. What can I do right now to cope with these emotions?

Activities

1. In your journal, write your answers to the "Questions to Ponder," focusing on what you can do now to move forward. Writing is similar to confession in its healing power. Capturing confusion in words on paper creates some sense of order and makes the situation less threatening.
2. If you haven't already done so, make an appointment with a health care center for an AIDS test and information on safe sex. Protect yourself!
3. Try this meditative exercise: Visualize yourself one year from today. Imagine yourself in a calm and peaceful state with the present pain gone. See yourself healed. Repeat this exercise whenever you feel discouraged.

Chapter 7: Family and Social Challenges

Questions to Ponder

1. What issues related to your mixed-orientation partnership trouble your family? Have your children reacted negatively? Are they accepting changes in the family dynamic? Take a step back and try to understand the overall effect of your partnership on close and extended family.
2. Assess your friendships and social life. Do you see gains or losses related to your changing relationship with your gay partner?
3. How do you feel about your gay mate now? Is friendship or closeness still possible?

Activity

Write in your journal a short description of your current relationship with your family, your gay partner, and your friends. Then write down what you would like those relationships to become. Imagine the very best outcome for all concerned and make an effort to bring it to fruition.

Chapter 8: Long-Term Personal Obstacles

Questions to Ponder

1. Do I recognize myself in any of these long-term challenges: loss of trust, reluctance to commit, religious or moral conflict?
2. Do I presently suffer from depression, bitterness, or loneliness?
3. Am I repeating old patterns that reiterate a past wound, or that perpetuate it?

Activities

1. Review the questions and self-help activities in Chapter 4. Using those exercises, work with your remaining issues.
2. Write in your journal any current challenges.
3. If you feel overwhelmed and unable to cope with these or other personal challenges, engage a counselor or therapist.

PART III: FRUITION—
THRIVING AFTER CRISIS

Chapter 9: Secrets of Transformation

Tools for Renewal

1. Take care of your health with plenty of exercise and a nutritious diet. A strong body is necessary to supply the energy needed for full emotional recovery.
2. "Relax as it is." Change the aspects of your situation that you have control over, but accept the things you cannot improve.
3. Keep talking. Use your confidant(e) or counselor as a safety valve for emotion. Feel your feelings and talk about them with a close friend or relative. Continue to write in your journal.
4. Get a pet. Having a living being to love and care for is therapeutic.
5. Use all available outside resources. Study this book and others that promote recovery. Search the Internet for information and support. Join a Straight Spouse Network chapter or use the Web site (www .straightspouse.org) to contact others who understand your experience.
6. Cultivate curiosity about the larger world. Develop new, constructive interests and activities that move you outside your personal problems. Take a class, start a new hobby, learn a new skill, or take a vacation to a place you've never seen.
7. When confidence allows, reach out to new friends who have a positive outlook. Avoid people who carry and reinforce anger and resentment.

Nourishing the Spirit

1. Let go of resentment.
2. Forgive.
3. Make amends to others for harm you've done, and then forgive yourself as well.
4. Accept what can't be changed; recognize the limits of your control over past situations.
5. Stay present in the present!

Appendix B

Related Resources

This resource list is offered to encourage straight spouses to continue their constructive path to recovery—with the suggestion to keep searching until satisfying answers emerge for personal questions. Many of these resources were used and recommended by people interviewed for this book.

ORGANIZATIONS

Children of Lesbians and Gays Everywhere (COLAGE)
1550 Bryant Street, Suite 830
San Francisco, CA 94103
Phone: 415-861-5437
Internet: COLAGE@colage.org

Support and information for children of gay, lesbian, bisexual, and transgender parents. Offers a web page, newsletter and pen pals.

Parents, Families, and Friends of Lesbians and Gays (PFLAG)
1726 M Street NW, Suite 400
Washington, DC 20036
Phone: 202-467-8180
Internet: www.pflag.org; info@pflag.org

Source of information and support for LGBT persons and family members.

Sexuality Information and Education Council of the United States (SIECUS)
130 W. 42nd Street, Suite 350
New York, NY 10036-7802
Phone: 212-819-9770
Internet: http://www.siecus.org/; siecus@siecus.org

When Your Spouse Comes Out
Published by The Haworth Press, Taylor & Francis Group, 2008. All rights reserved.
doi:10.1300/6046_11

139

Distributes information on sexuality, including "Quick facts on Religion and Sexuality."

Straight Spouse Network (SSN)
P.O. Box 507
Mahwah, NJ 07430-2236
Phone: 201-825-7512 (SSN Office); 510-595-1005 (Support and Media)
Internet: http://www.straightspouse.org; dir@straightspouse.org

Offers resources specific to mixed-orientation couples and straight spouses or partners, current or former, of gay, lesbian, bisexual, or transgender mates.

INTERNET MAILING LISTS

BABES Network
http://www.babesnetwork.org/

Dedicated to building community among women from all walks of life who are facing HIV and AIDS. A program of the YWCA in Seattle, BABES offers a monthly bilingual newsletter, support, advocacy, and information.

MMTL—Men Married to Lesbians
http://groups.yahoo.com/group/MMTL/

Closed membership support group for men who are married to lesbian or bisexual women, who are seeking help in coping with the challenges of a mixed-orientation marriage, and who desire more positive relationships with their spouses.

Spouse Support Mailing List for Mixed Orientation Marriages (SSML-MOR)
http://www.ssml-mor.org

Mailing list for heterosexual spouses and/or gay, lesbian, or bisexual spouses in mixed-orientation marriages who want constructive resolutions for relationship problems and wish to restore and maintain positive relationships with their spouses.

str8s
http://www.mailinglist.net/str8s/

Closed, private subscription mailing list limited to straight spouses of bisexual, gay, or lesbian partners. Emphasizes positive outcomes, whether couples stay together or not.

We Are Wildflowers
http://www.wearewildflowers.com/

Support for women who have been or who are currently married to LDS (Mormon) gay men.

Wives of Bi/Gay Husbands
http://groups.yahoo.com/group/WivesofBiGayHusbands/

A closed membership online support group for straight wives of bi/gay/SSA/trans men. Offers understanding and empathy to its more than 2,000 members, encouraging each woman to decide her own course toward healing. Accessible through a link on the Straight Spouse Network site: www.straightspouse.org.

AIDS INFORMATION

Centers for Disease Control, AIDS Division
http://www.cdc.gov/hiv/dhap.htm

A division of the U.S. Department of Health and Human Services. Provides extensive information on HIV infection, including sections on prevention, statistics, current studies, journal articles, publications, and frequently asked questions. Focus is on prevention, encouraging persons at high risk for HIV to change and maintain behaviors to avoid infection. New strategies also aim at early diagnosis and increased access to quality medical care and treatment.

National AIDS Hotline
1-800-342-AIDS (24-hour hotline)
Spanish speaking: 1-800-344-7432
TDD: 1-800-243-7889

A listing of direct phone numbers for diverse organizations serving individuals and families affected by HIV/AIDS. A section of The Body: The Complete HIV/AIDS Resource, whose mission is to use the Web to lower barriers between patients and clinicians, demystify HIV/AIDS and its treatment, improve patients' quality of life, and foster community through human connection. Emphasizes prevention, testing, treatment, living with AIDS, and connecting to others. Links lead to additional resources in both English and Spanish.

National Pediatric AIDS Network
http://www.npan.org/

Resource for information on HIV/AIDS, especially in young people. See "HIV: The Basics."

BOOKS

Beattie, Melody. *Beyond Codependency.* New York: Harper and Row, 1989. The chapter "Overcoming Fatal Attractions" is especially recommended.

Bozett, Frederick W. and Sussman, M.B., eds. *Homosexuality and Family Relations.* Binghamton, NY: Harrington Park Press, 1988. A collection of articles on family relationship issues.

Buxton, Amity Pierce. *The Other Side of the Closet: The Coming-Out Crisis for Straight Spouses and Families,* Revised Edition. New York: Wiley, 1994. Originally published in 1991, this is a study of family trauma right after disclosure, based on research by an experienced counselor.

Clark, Donald Henry. *The New Loving Someone Gay,* Revised Edition. Berkeley, CA: Celestial Arts, 1997. Written by a gay clinical psychologist, the emphasis is on dispelling prejudices and confusion about homosexuality. Its focus is on the gay partner, not on the straight spouse.

Corley, Andre. *The Final Closet: The Gay Parent's Guide for Coming Out to Their Children.* Miami, FL: Editech, 1990. Discusses appropriate ways to talk with children about homosexuality.

Garner, Abigail. *Families Like Mine: Children of Gay Parents Tell It Like It Is.* New York: HarperCollins, 2004. Offers stories from grown children of gay and lesbian parents. Good for parents needing basic advice and older adolescents needing to understand their unique experience.

Gillespie, Janet. *Diverse Families, Competent Families.* Binghamton, NY: The Haworth Press, 1999. Written for professional caregivers; offers insight and approaches for working with topics that include LGBT, ethnic, and economic issues.

Gochros, Jean Schaar. *When Husbands Come Out of the Closet.* Binghamton, NY: The Haworth Press, 1989. A thorough, academic approach to the subject of women with gay or bisexual partners.

Grever, Carol. *My Husband Is Gay: A Woman's Guide to Surviving the Crisis.* Berkeley, CA: Crossing Press, 2001. Personal stories of twenty-six women provide guidance in facing the immediate coming-out crisis.

Hill, Ivan. *The Bisexual Spouse.* New York: Harper, 1987. Explores ethical issues raised by bisexuality within marriage.

Kaye, Bonnie. *Is He Straight? A Checklist for Women Who Wonder.* Lincoln, NE: iUniverse.com, 2000. Self-help book for women who suspect that their husbands are gay.

Laird, Joan and Green, Robert-Jay. *Lesbians and Gays in Couples and Families: A Handbook for Therapists.* San Francisco, CA: Jossey-Bass, 1996. Displays scholarship and clinical wisdom in a long collection of essays aimed primarily at professionals but also useful as a reference.

Lerner, Harriet. *Life Preservers: Staying Afloat in Love and Life.* New York: HarperCollins, 1996. Addresses the straight spouse dilemma, among other life challenges.

Marcus, Eric. *Is It a Choice?,* Revised Edition. New York: HarperCollins, 1999. Answers 300 frequently asked questions about gay and lesbian people.

Pearson, Carol Lynn. *Goodbye, I Love You.* New York: Jove, 1989. Autobiographical account by a Mormon woman whose husband comes out, leaves the marriage, then returns home to be nursed by his ex-wife through his final illness with AIDS.

Rosenberg, Marshall. *Nonviolent Communication: A Language of Life.* Encinitas, CA: PuddleDancer Press, 2005. How to communicate respectfully, compassionately, and effectively in ways that support full living.

Shulman, Diana. *Co-Parenting After Divorce: How to Raise Happy, Healthy Children in Two-Home Families.* Sherman Oaks, CA: WinnSpeed Press, 1996. How-to guide offering help with the common problems and conflicts of co-parenting.

Snow, Judith. *How It Feels to Have a Gay or Lesbian Parent: A Book By Kids for Kids of All Ages.* Binghamton, NY: The Haworth Press, 2004.

Stories that help children, adolescents, and adults understand the child and adolescent experience.

Strock, Carren. *Married Women Who Love Women*. New York: Doubleday, 1998. Based on personal experience and 100 interviews, it explores the subject of married women dealing with lesbian desires.

Teyber, Edward. *Helping Children Cope with Divorce*. New York: John Wiley and Sons Press, 2001. Named one of the Ten Best Parenting Books of the Year by *Child Magazine*. Offers a detailed program for parents to support every member of the family in this situation.

Whitney, Catherine. *Uncommon Lives: Gay Men and Straight Women*. Columbus, OH: New American Press, 1990. Focuses on unorthodox alternative family units and their challenges.

FILMS

One Gay, One Straight: Complicated Marriages. DVD. Directed by Roslyn Dauber, produced by Carol Grever. Dauber Film Services, 2007. Available at www.carolgrever.com.

References

AARP (2005). *Sexuality at Midlife and Beyond: 2004 Update of Attitudes and Behaviors.* Available: http://assets.aarp.org/rgcenter/general/2004_sexuality.pdf.

American Psychiatric Association (1994). *Diagnostic and Statistical Manual of Mental Disorders,* Fourth Edition. Washington, DC: American Psychiatric Association.

Bowman, Deborah and Leakey, Trish (2006). The Power of Gestalt Therapy in Accessing the Transpersonal: Working with Physical Difference and Disability. *Gestalt Review, 10*(1): 42-59.

Cass, Vivienne C. (1979). Homosexual Identity Formation: A Theoretical Model. *Journal of Homosexuality, 4*(3): 219-235.

Cass, Vivienne C. (1984). Homosexual Identity Formation: Testing a Theoretical Model. *Journal of Sex Research,* (20): 143-167.

Eisenberger, Naomi L. and Lieberman, Matthew D. (2003). Does Rejection Hurt? An fMRI Study of Social Exclusion. *Science, 302*(5643): 290-292.

Erikson, Erik H. (1950). *Childhood and Society.* New York: W.W. Norton and Company, Inc.

Erikson, Erik H. (1968). *Identity: Youth and Crisis.* New York: W.W. Norton and Company, Inc.

Garner, Abigail (2005). *Families Like Mine: Children of Gay Parents Tell It Like It Is.* New York: Harper.

Grever, Carol (2001). *My Husband Is Gay: A Woman's Guide to Surviving the Crisis.* Berkeley, CA: Crossing Press.

Heller, Sharon (1997). *The Vital Touch.* New York: Henry Holt and Company, LLC.

Kübler-Ross, Elisabeth (1969). *On Death and Dying.* New York: Touchstone.

Kübler-Ross, Elisabeth and Kessler, David (2005). *On Grief and Grieving: Finding the Meaning of Grief through the 5 Stages of Loss.* Elizabeth Kübler Ross Family Limited Partnership and David Kessler, Inc. New York: Scribner.

LeDoux, Joseph (1996). *The Emotional Brain: The Mysterious Underpinnings of Emotional Life.* New York: Touchstone.

Maslow, Abraham (1968). *Toward a Psychology of Being.* New York: John Wiley and Sons, Inc.

Perls, Frederick, Ralph Hefferline, and Paul Goodman (1951). *Gestalt Therapy Integrated: Contours of Theory and Practice.* New York: Random House.

When Your Spouse Comes Out
Published by The Haworth Press, Taylor & Francis Group, 2008. All rights reserved.
doi:10.1300/6046_12

PFLAG, Task Force for Spouses and Children of Lesbians and Gay Men (2006). *Opening the Straight Spouse's Closet*. Washington, DC: Parents, Families and Friends of Lesbians and Gays.

Polster, Erving and Murian Polster (1973). *Gestalt Therapy Integrated: Contours of Theory and Practice*. New York: Bantam Books.

Rosenberg, Marshall (2005). *Nonviolent Communication: A Language of Life*. California: PuddleDancer Press.

Snow, Judith E. (2004). *How It Feels to Have a Gay or Lesbian Parent: A Book by Kids for Kids of All Ages*. Binghamton, NY: The Haworth Press.

UNAIDS (Joint United Nations Programme on HIV/AIDS) (2006). *UNAIDS 2006 Report on the Global AIDS Epidemic*. www.unaids.org.

Index

Page numbers followed by the letter "f" indicate figures.

When Your Spouse Comes Out
Published by The Haworth Press, Taylor & Francis Group, 2008. All rights reserved.
doi:10.1300/6046_13
147